First Ownership Of OHIO LANDS

By
Albion Morris Dyer, A.M.

Southern Historical Press, Inc.
Greenville, South Carolina

This volume was reproduced
from a personal copy located in
the Publishers private library

All rights reserved. No part of this publication may be reproduced,
stored in a retrieval system, transmitted in any form, posted
on the web in any form or by any means without the
prior written permission of the publisher.

Please direct all correspondence and book orders to:
SOUTHERN HISTORICAL PRESS, Inc.
1071 Park West Blvd.
Greenville, SC 29611

Published 1911:
   New England Historic Genealogical Society
   Boston, MA.
ISBN #978-1-63914-676-5
Printed in the United States of America

FIRST OWNERSHIP OF OHIO LANDS

At the end of the war of the American Revolution the Continental Congress came into possession of certain western lands, surrendered by the British Crown to the United States in the treaty signed at Paris on the 3d day of September, 1783. The "crown lands," as they were called, lay back of the heads of the Atlantic rivers and over the mountains, extending westward to the distant Father of Waters. They were known to the colonies as the "back lands" or "back country," and being waste and uncultivated, remote from the ships and barred by many hazards, were not especially desirable in the early settlements. Here wars had raged for unknown centuries, and war was to linger for many years. Two great savage nations had fought from the beginning for this vast wilderness, and three European powers had striven from its discovery to possess it. Finally it was won from the French by the united arms of the King and colonies and joined to Quebec to enter upon a new epoch. Afterwards the crown lands appear in the public councils of the colonies, and that part lying beyond the Ohio River is referred to in the early records as "The Western Territory," a term obviously too broad, since there was western territory on both sides of the river. Under this name it passed for many years, both in and out of Congress; but the official designation of the region was changed in the final action on the famous Ordinance of 1787, where, in the last reading, the title was extended to "The Territory of the United States North-West of the River Ohio."[1] Such is the origin of the Northwest Territory, nursery of states, first extension in area of the United States, first grand resource of the nation, yielding the first considerable item of revenue in the public accounts.

The Northwest Territory passed to the United States indisputably, as part of the lands embraced within the boundary line established by Article III of the Treaty of Paris, reading: "through the middle of the lakes, and along the middle of the river Mississippi, until it shall intersect the northern-most part of the thirty-first degree of north latitude." The English right thus descending to the United States included the relinquished rights of Spain and France, and the King of France had confirmed the transfer by separate treaties giving up forever to the Americans all his claims west of the Mississippi. No other civilized power laid claim to these lands, yet no territory of state ever had more troublesome encumbrances. Four colonies had covered the property with overlapping titles based on vague royal grants and Indian treaties. The territorial land rights of these and other states were advocated by the commissioners of Congress in the negotiation of peace with England, as the basis of a demand for the territory, and the United States was further bound to respect the claims of the states by a specific clause of the articles of confederation. Many tribes of Indians occupied the territory as hereditary owners, and their right of habitation had been confirmed to them by royal proclamation. Relying upon this confirmation a part of the inhabitants had allied themselves with the British

---

[1] Printed copies of the Ordinance of 1787, preserved in the Library of Congress, No. 30, Papers of the Continental Congress, show alterations made at various stages of its progress. The first use of the limitation in the title seems to be on the date of passage, July 13, 1787, but it is some time before "Northwest Territory" was in general use.

cause against the Americans for the retention of their homes and hunting grounds, while the other part of the Indians had remained neutral or assisted the colonies. The hostile Indians were not yet subdued; they were still in armed possession of the frontier, while the friendly tribes could not well be disturbed in their wigwams without serious consequences. Added to this were several minor complications: pledges of bounty land to the military; indeterminate grants within the territory to independent companies; squatter inroads into the bottoms of the Ohio; and British garrisons keeping guard at the outposts supposedly encouraging natives in hostilities, and furnishing aid and comfort to intruders. These conflicting elements were cleared away from the title by good management of Congress, and the United States was able to establish a hold on the Northwest Territory. With great patience, exercising powers assumed but not granted, the American states solved their first political problem, the land issue, quieted the discordant states and gloriously concluded the confederacy. In the course of this business through the assembly, with wonderful enlightenment and in marvellous wisdom of counsels, the title of the Northwest Territory was cleared; the frontier was made safe and the Indians protected within their own property limits under permanent relations of ward-ship; a public domain was created and a rational system of surveying devised to open it; a sinking fund was started, which in time extinguished the whole state and federal debt; and a mode was provided for the extension of settlements on the territory, and for the expansion of the American system of representative government under the flag.

It is not the present purpose of the writer to trace the factors of this first nationalizing movement in American history. The plan in this preliminary sketch is merely to link together events in the course of action which cleared the title to the Northwest Territory, and to follow with more detail the subsequent steps by which Congress established an open doorway into the West. That open door was Ohio. Between the meridians confining this great state the problem of the preparation of a seat in the wilderness for civilization was worked out on heroic lines. These matters are of more than local interest, although the details may not be found in the larger histories.

Years before the crown lands had passed to the United States, four of the states "claiming to the Mississippi or South Sea," assumed sovereign rights of preëmption of soil and jurisdiction over the lands comprising the Northwest Territory. Massachusetts and Connecticut rested their title on royal charters, claiming parallel strips of land which cut off the northern part of the Territory. New York claimed by the historic deed of the Six Nations, and her title covered nearly the whole extent of the country south of the lakes. Virginia's proofs were in the royal grants and European treaties, supported by the subsequent military achievement of Clark, and her claims overspread everything from the Canadas far into the South. The claims of the Carolinas and of Georgia were of the same nature, but they fell below the Ohio River. The proofs upon which many if not all of these claims rested had never been tested by legal examination or comparison. In some instances the charters or treaties were of uncertain force and effect. The claims themselves were plainly conflicting. The delineations in the documentary proofs were vague and inaccurate, and the descriptions were based on erroneous geographical knowledge. It was obvious from the first that difficulties would arise in settling these claims, but it was no time in the midst of uncertain war for sister states to dispute over unconquered territory, nor to search for boundaries in a wilderness not yet rid of the savage allies of the King. Moreover the lands were still crown property, and there was no hope of possessing them save "through the common sword, purse and blood of all the colonies united in one common effort." Under the circumstances the claimant states were disposed to rest on their theoretical rights, awaiting the outcome of the Revolution. They worked together in the prosecution of the war without thought of their conflicting claims, and they even engaged to enter into a perpetual union with the lesser colonies, as into a "firm league of friendship," utterly unmindful of the trouble sure to come when boundaries were defined and the limits of jurisdiction determined.

This complacent policy of undisputed, undisturbed ownership of the crown lands by neighborly colonies might have continued unbroken throughout the period of war, but one of the claimants, more "ambitiously grasping for territories" than the others, made presumptions under her charters that destroyed amity and planted discord among the states. Virginia was the direct cause of the fear and distrust, and Maryland led the opposition. Presuming upon the validity of untried proofs of title, and confident of enforcing her indeterminate claims, the Old Dominion entered upon a course of action in the summer of 1776, which, if followed out to its conclusion, would not only exclude the smaller colonies from participation in the benefits of the property but would place all her neighbors, great and small, in position of trespassers. Unexpectedly, in the midst of general alarms of British invasion, with union still in the balance and independence not yet declared, the Virginians advanced pretensions to jurisdiction and actual possession of all lands and waters of the region between the Chesapeake frontage and the Mississippi River, warning off intruders, and announcing intentions of setting up dependent territorial governments westward of the Alleghany Mountains. Maryland spoke up boldly against these arrogant presumptions of her powerful trans-Potomac neighbor, and so started a controversy which increased the embarrassments of Congress in the conduct of the war, and placed the cause of independence in greatest jeopardy. Maryland held to the demand for complete neutralization of the public lands on principles of fairness, if not of right; and, by constant insistance, at the risk of wrecking the Union, she broke down the plans of Virginia and opened the way for the cessions of all the western country.

The origin of the controversy over the crown lands may be said to be in the adoption of the "Constitution and Form of Government" agreed to in general convention of the delegates and representatives of the several counties and corporations of Virginia, held at the capitol, in the city of Williamsburg, on the 6th of May, 1776. A paragraph of the constitution reads as follows:

> The territories contained within the charters erecting the colonies of Maryland, Pennsylvania, North and South Carolina, are hereby ceded, released, and forever confirmed to the people of those colonies respectively, with all the rights of property, jurisdiction and government, and all other rights whatsoever, which might at any time hereafter have been claimed by Virginia, except the free navigation and use of the rivers Potomack and Pocomoke, with the property of the Virginia shore and strands bordering on either of the said rivers, and all improvements which have been or shall be made thereon. The western and northern extent of Virginia shall, in all other respects, stand as fixed by the charter of King James the First, in the year one thousand six hundred and nine, and by public Treaty of Peace between the courts of Great Britain and France in the year one thousand seven hundred and sixty-three; unless, by act of legislature, one or more territories shall hereafter be laid off, and governments estab-

lished westward of the Allegeny mountains. And no purchase of lands shall be made of the Indian natives, but on behalf of the public, by authority of the general assembly.

Maryland unhesitatingly pronounced this claim in the constitution of Virginia as "injurious to the inhabitants of this state." At the convention of delegates of Maryland in session at Annapolis, October 29, 1776, it was ordered by a vote and resolve that this paragraph of the Virginia Constitution be read, and it was read and spread upon the minutes of the convention. Whereupon it was resolved "That this convention will on tomorrow resolve itself into a committee of the whole; to take the same into consideration." The following day, October 30, according to the order of the day, the objectionable paragraph was considered. After some time spent thereon the committee reported several resolutions by which the convention of the state of Maryland declared unanimously that Virginia had no title to any territory included in the charter granted to the baron of Baltimore, and that the waters of that part of the Chesapeake included in the charter ought to be considered as a common highway free for the people of the bordering states, and they further resolved unanimously:

That it is the opinion of this convention, that the very extensive claim of the state of Virginia to the back lands hath no foundation in justice, and that if the same or any like claim be admitted, the freedom of the smaller states and the liberties of America may be thereby greatly endangered; this convention being firmly persuaded, that if the dominion over these lands should be established by the blood and treasure of the United States, such lands ought to be considered as the common stock, to be parcelled out at proper times into convenient, free and independent governments.

It does not appear in the resolutions what means were contemplated by the convention of Maryland to bring this opinion to bear upon the "arrogance" of her neighbor, but within ten days of the passage of the resolutions, November 10th, to be exact, Maryland delegates were appointed in the convention to represent the state in Congress with expressed power "to concur with the other United States, or a majority or them, in forming a confederation, providing that such confederation, when formed, be not binding upon this state without the assent of the general assembly."

No one would be inclined to doubt that the Maryland delegation was sent to Congress charged with the responsibility of engrafting this principle of national disposition of the public territory upon the fundamental plan of confederacy then in process of formation in Philadelphia. There is no documentary commission to show this and the recorded proceedings of the state and congressional assemblies are so meagre and incomplete that inferences may not always be drawn from them with safety. But the steps taken by the Marylanders are so clear and distinct, both in the home assembly and in the general congress, that they indicate a settled plan to determine all matter of territorial ownership and boundaries before confederating with the claimant colonies.[2]

[2]The sentiments of Maryland thus vigorously expressed regarding the grasping disposition of Virginia, were inflamed at the time by misunderstanding of the offer of land for bounty in the raising of eighty-eight battalions of troops called for by the continental board of war in September, 1776. Considering this matter in October the convention formally resolved to raise the eight battalions assigned to Maryland, but, declining to countenance the promise of land where there was no land to give, substituted an offer of ten dollars cash for each enlistment in lieu of the hundred acres pledged by Congress. This action evoked criticism in Congress, in the form of a resolution adopted October 30, the exact date of the Maryland resolve against the Virginia constitution, recommending a reconsideration of the cash bounty substitution, on the theory thus expressed:

It was not in the stated programme of Congress to introduce the land claims into the confederation debates. In fact it was the bounden duty of the leaders of Congress to exclude this subject from the discussion, as well as from the plan of confederacy, owing to primary considerations. No reference to the lands appears in the original Franklin sketch of a plan of government read in Congress, July 21, 1775. But in the committee's draft substituted a year later, a mode of treatment of indeterminate boundary lines and conflicting territorial land claims is provided. In this second draft there is a clause reading: "When the boundaries of any colony shall be ascertained by agreement all the other colonies shall guaranty to such colony the full and peaceable possession of, and the full and entire jurisdiction in, and over the territories included within such boundaries." And among the powers of Congress enumerated are the following:

Limiting the bounds of these colonies which, by charter or proclamation, or under any pretence, are said to extend to the south sea and ascertaining those bounds of any other colony that appears to be indeterminate: Assigning territories for new colonies, either in lands to be thus separated from colonies and hereafter purchased, or obtained by the crown of Great Britain from the Indians, or hereafter to be purchased or obtained from them: Disposing of all such lands for the general benefit of all the United Colonies: Ascertaining boundaries of such new colonies within which forms of government are to be established on principles of liberty.

These clauses were not presented as a part of the committee's substitute. They were the ideas of Mr. Dickinson and were merely "submitted to congress," very likely on his own responsibility. They were probably not

---

That the said convention, by their said resolution, seem to apprehend that their state would be obliged, in their individual capacity, to make good the bounty of land hereafter to be given to the soldiery; whereas it was the intention of congress to provide the said land at the expense of the United States.

But this assurance served only to confuse Maryland. The convention took up the former resolution for raising the quota of troops, and "on a very deliberate and attentive consideration of the subject," came to certain resolutions, of the date of November 9, informing Congress of the precise opinion of Maryland on the offer of land, which are in part as follows:

If the bounty of land should be offered as proposed to individuals of this quota, this state would be bound in good faith to see that bounty effectually granted, and therefore as this state has no lands belonging solely and exclusively to itself, with which to make good the bounty, it is not only prudent, but necessary, before they do an act which will engage the faith of this state, to know what land is to be applied, and on what terms, to the designated purpose.

That this convention are under the strongest impressions that the back lands claimed by the British Crown, if secured by the blood and treasure of all, ought in reason, justice, and policy, to be considered as common stock, to be parcelled out by congress into free, convenient, and independent governments, as the wisdom of that body shall hereafter direct; but if these (the only lands as this convention apprehend that can) should be provided by congress at the expense of the United States to make good the proffered bounties, every idea of their being a common stock must be therefore given up: some of the states may, by fixing their own price on the land, pay off what of their quota of the public debt they please, and have their extensive territory settled by the soldiery of the other states, whilst this state and a few others must be so weakened and impoverished, that they can hold their liberties only at the will of their powerful neighbors.

Under these impressions the Maryland convention issued instructions to the enlistment commissioners to repair to the camps and endeavor to enlist such troops and militia of the state as were willing to enter into the continental service on the terms proposed by Congress

... immediately on its being made known to them that the honourable congress will specify any land belonging to the United States as a common stock to be divided amongst the soldiery in their service ... but if the honourable congress will not specify the lands as aforesaid ... they shall endeavour to effect the said enlistment on the bounty of twenty dollars allowed by congress; but they are not to engage the faith of this state to give or make good any bounty of lands, or give any assurance whatsoever that they will have such bounty.

Congress not being able to make such specification, and evidently wishing to avoid a discussion of the theory of land claims quieted the trouble of Maryland for the time being by an order dated November 13, instructing the president to inform the convention:

That if the inhabitants of that state will inlist to serve during the present war, they already have the faith of the United States of America pledged for the land.

considered by Congress and were promptly expunged from the draft. They do not appear again, nor anything like them anywhere in tentative or finished form. It was the settled policy of Congress to avoid the subject of the territories, and this principle prevailed from first to last.

But the confederation discussions in Congress soon offered an opportunity for the Maryland delegation to interject the subject of western lands. The matter came up logically in the course of consideration of the draft of an article of the confederation relating to the powers of Congress. This discussion followed a prolonged debate on fixing a suitable criterion of taxation to meet the costs of war, a feature of the constitution that caused considerable trouble in the succeeding years. In the Franklin draft framed in 1775, public money for war expenses was to be raised by a simple poll tax. But subsesequent drafts elaborated the rule, enlarging its scope, and extending its application to cover back outlays for war expenses. When the article relating to taxation was taken up in its final discussion, October 9, 1777, further differences of opinion developed among the delegates; the population tax was dropped, and a general property tax was proposed. This was burning ground; expenditures of the individual colonies in the early stages of the war before Congress had introduced the general machinery of finance. The debate dragged along through four days' sessions and doubtless something was said that aroused the old grudge and stirred up the spirit of contention. The taxation debate terminated on the 14th of October in agreement on a form of Article VIII as it stands in the finished plan of confederacy, basing taxation on "the value of all land within each state granted to or surveyed for any person, as such land the buildings and improvements thereon shall be estimated."[3]

In the next day's session, October 15, came the land question in the form of resolutions proposing national control of the western territory. The question may have come from the Maryland delegation, but this is not certain. Three resolutions were read in succession presenting the proposition in different forms. The authorship of the resolutions is not stated in the record, but it is probable that one, if not all, was the means adopted by the Marylanders for fulfilling their instructions from the convention issued the year before. The first resolution proposed:

That in order to render the present confederacy firm and perpetual, it is essential that the limits of each respective territorial jurisdiction should be ascertained by the articles of confederation, and therefore, it is recommended to the legislatures of every state to lay before Congress a description of the territorial lands of each of their respective states, and a summary of the grants, treaties and proofs upon which they are claimed or established.

It might be supposed that this reasonable proposition would have gained the support of the smaller colonies whose interests it especially favored, but on this occasion, as throughout the controversy, the smaller states were not united. New Hampshire, Rhode Island, and New Jersey opposed the resolution, while New York, Pennsylvania, and Maryland supported it

[3] The rule of taxation provided for in Article VIII of the confederation proved to be inconvenient and uncertain, especially in its retrospective application. The states could not come to terms in regard to what early expenditures ought to be allowed by Congress and paid out of the public treasury. In consequence Article VIII was presented to Congress for amendment and a substitute was submitted to the states for ratification in April, 1783, by which the abandoned population tax was restored, but in a modified form. This was the first attempt to change the fundamental law of the Union, and in it may be found some interesting and suggestive traces of the color line and sectionalism.

Delaware and Georgia were not represented, and the vote stood eight to three. No division is given in the record of vote on the second amendment, and the third received the solitary support of Maryland, the vote of New Jersey being divided. Following are the second and third amendments:

The United States in Congress assembled shall have the sole and exclusive right and power to ascertain and fix the western boundary of such states as claim to the South Sea, and to dispose of all land beyond the boundary so ascertained, for the benefit of the United States.

The United States in Congress assembled shall have the sole and exclusive right and power to ascertain and fix the western boundary of such states as claim to the Mississippi or South Sea, and lay out the land beyond the boundary so ascertained into separate and independent states, from time to time, as the number and circumstances of the people may require.[4]

There is nothing in the record to show how these three resolutions were received by Congress, although it appears that they were handled without much "consideration" or discussion. Probably the three amendments were summarily rejected in succession with little or no debate. There was some complaint of this mode of Congressional procedure in the subsequent controversy, and it is recorded afterwards, relative to similar propositions, that "they involve questions, the discussion of which was declined on mature consideration when the articles of confederation were debated."[5] Virginia pointed out the inconsistency of this doctrine with the principles upon which the boundaries of the United States were described in an ultimatum in the terms of peace soon afterwards placed in negotiation with England:

The United States could hold no territory but in right of some one individual state in the Union. Any argument fairly urged to prove that any particular tract of country, within the limits claimed by Congress on behalf of the United States, is not a part of the chartered territory of some one of them, must militate with equal force against the right of the United States in general; and tend to prove such tract of country (if northwest of the Ohio river) part of the British province of Canada.[6]

It would be idle to conjecture as to the effect of those resolutions had they gone into the plan of confederation. It might be that the confines of the United States would have been at the mountains, as Virginia suggested would be the case, and the region between the Great Lakes and the Ohio might have remained until now a part of the Dominion of Canada. The only appreciable effect of their introduction at this time was in the action

[4] Herbert B. Adams, in his Maryland's Influence in Founding a National Commonwealth, a pamphlet published by the Maryland Historical Society, 1877, credits the third amendment of October 15, 1777, to Maryland. He states, in italics, by way of proof: "*Only Maryland voted in the affirmative*," but offers no other support of the assertion. Mr. Adams adds: "But in this motion was suggested that idea of political expansion under sovereign control of Congress, which ultimately prevailed and constituted upon grounds of necessity, a truly National Republic: Not only the suggestion of a firm lasting union upon the basis of a territorial commonwealth, but the chief influence in founding such a union, must be ascribed to Maryland. . . . . The original proposition that Congress should exercise sovereign power over the western country was a pioneer thought, or, as the Germans say a *bahnrechende Idee*" (p. 28). This interesting suggesion might have been made with equal warrant respecting the earlier Maryland expression, the opinion of the Annapolis convention pronounced October 30, 1776; if not indeed of the Virginia Constitution of May, 1776, which carried the idea of ultra-montane territorial dependencies afterwards elaborated in the Ordinance of 1787.

[5] Sept. 6, 1780. Journals of Congress.

[6] From the Virginia Remonstrance. This document and others relating to this matter are printed in full in Hening's Virginia Statutes at Large, vol. 10, p. 547.

which followed. The larger states took alarm from this attack upon their cherished rights, and they voted to insert in the draft a clause which does not appear in any earlier form, an addition to Article IX, reading: "No state shall be deprived of territory for the benefit of the United States." The claimant states placed this in the law of the confederacy on October 27, by which they alarmed others of the smaller colonies and laid the basis for subsequent loss of territory they sought to safeguard.

The plan of confederation as finally agreed upon in Congress, Saturday November 15, 1777, contained no reference to vacant land, or western boundaries except the saving clause introduced at the last to satisfy the larger states. No time was lost in placing the plan before the thirteen states for conclusion. The articles of confederation were revised and arranged, and three hundred copies were printed. A circular letter addressed to the states to accompany the articles of confederation was prepared by a committee appointed to the task. Thirteen copies of the letter were made out and signed by the president of Congress, and on Monday, November 17, these two documents were transmitted to the executive authorities of the several states. The letter of address is a dignified plea to hasten the conclusion of confederation. The articles were earnestly recommended to the immediate and dispassionate attention of the legislatures, with expressions of appology for expecting that any plan should exactly correspond with the maxims and political views of every particular state, regret at the time which had elapsed in preparing the plan for consideration, and solicitude as to the time which must be necessarily spent before it can be ratified. The legislatures were recommended "to invest their delegates with powers to subscribe articles of confederation, and to attend congress for that purpose on or before the 10th day of March next."

The states received the plan and address early in December, in ample time for the necessary action in the assemblies before the day set for ratification in Congress. But it does not seem that they were especially affected by the urgent plea for haste. Virginia alone made prompt reply. The general assembly of that state complied immediately with all recommendations of the address. Without stopping for debate, and without division, each house of the assembly approved the articles and ratified them with resolutions calling for speedy conclusion of confederation. The enabling act of Virginia bears date of December 16, 1777,[7] scarce a month from the date of the address. Surely the Old Dominion was well satisfied with the plan. Other states were not so well pleased. They were all as anxious for confederacy and union as a means of ending the war, but they were not in a hurry to ratify. Most of the states found fault with the plan. They framed objections calling for amendments, and forwarded them to their delegates for presentation to Congress. Several states waited long for changes to be made. The responses of the legislatures show the extent and nature of the dissatisfaction with the terms proposed for confederation.

The date set for ratification, March 10, 1778, was permitted to pass by without the ceremony called for in the programme. Not enough delegates had received the expected powers and instructions, called for in the letter of address, to justify an attempt to proceed with confederation, and so matters

---

[7] The published Journals of Congress print this enabling act of the Virginia assembly under date of Dec. 15, 1778. This error has come from the MS. vol. 9 (History of Confederation), p. 123, Papers of the Continental Congress, Library of Congress. There is an error also in the text of the act—the date of the adoption of the articles of confederation by Congress being "The 17th day of November last," instead of the 7th as it is there given.

drifted along while the states deliberated. Information travelled slowly then and people were not so ready to spread news. Georgia, for example, took action on the plan of confederation in February, and the result of the action was not reported until the 23d of July. But it must have been known among the delegates that objections had been raised in many of the legislatures against the plan proposed, and no doubt much anxiety was felt as to the fate of the confederacy.

Congress, then in session at Yorktown, was not disposed to begin the canvass of accumulating objections until forced into considering them by the sudden demands of the Maryland delegation. Fresh instructions just received from home called for immediate notice. The general assembly of Maryland on Saturday the 20th of June, 1778, resolved:

> That the delegates from this state to Congress consider themselves bound by the instructions given in October session last, and that they endeavor to procure from Congress an explicit answer to the propositions therein contained; but that they do not at any time consider themselves at liberty to ratify or confirm any confederation of perpetual friendship and union, until they have communicated such answer to the general assembly of this state and shall receive their express authority to do so.

The next Monday, June 22, after the issue of these explicit instructions, Congress having proceeded to consider the objections to the articles of confederation, the delegates from Maryland read to Congress these instructions, and moved "that the objections from the state of Maryland be immediately taken up and considered by congress, that the delegates from Maryland may transmit to that state, with all possible despatch, the determination of congress on these objections." The motion being put and resolved in the affirmative, three objections of Maryland were read and voted upon out of the regular order of roll call, which should have begun with New Hampshire.

The canvas of returns from the legislatures of the thirteen states as recorded in the Journals of Congress under date of June 22 to 26, 1778, shows only three states approving of the articles "as they now stand," New Hampshire, New York, and Virginia. A fourth had likewise approved, but the official report from North Carolina did not arrive until after the canvas was concluded. Objections had been received by delegates of eight states and Delaware was still to be heard from. South Carolina sent twenty-three alterations, and Rhode Island, "having had the articles repeatedly read, and having maturely weighed and most seriously deliberated upon them as their importance deserves," sent along three amendments, with powers to her delegates "to accede to and sign the articles provided they be acceded to by eight of the other states." The objections were numerous and scattering. They were mostly in the form of verbal changes of little, if any, interest to-day.[8] The more important criticism came from four states in the form of a presentment against the land policy of the claimant states.

The method of consideration applied by Congress to these objections deserves a passing notice. According to the records in the Journals of Congress parts of three days in the midst of other business served to dispose of them all. Very little time was given to the separate objections. The roll

---

[8] Massachusetts and Connecticut expressed their dissatisfaction with the article relating to taxation. The former proposed "That the rule of apportionment of taxation be varied from time to time, until experience shall have showed what rule of apportionment will be most equal and consequently just." Connecticut asked to change the basis of taxation from the lands to "the number of inhabitants in each state."

was called geographically, except that Maryland came first, and the objections from the state called were read by the delegates. Sometimes there was debate, but debate was slow. One elaborate series of objections pertaining to widely different features of the confederation were grouped into one motion and cast out by a single division. Another set of belated objections were, apparently, disregarded entirely. In this fashion the business was rushed through, and on the third day Congress was able to report that the articles, "after mature deliberation, had been adopted, without amendment."

Two of the objections filed by the Maryland delegates do not concern this inquiry as they pertain to other matters, but the third brought up the contention on the land question in still another form. By this an explanation was called for of the obnoxious safety clause in Article IX. The Maryland assembly expressed dissatisfaction with this clause and demanded the addition of the following:

The United States in Congress assembled shall have the power to appoint commissioners, who shall be fully authorized and empowered to ascertain and restrict the boundaries of such of the confederated states which claim to extend to the river Mississippi, or South Sea.

This amendment received attention during two sessions of Congress, and although it failed of passage the solitary vote of Maryland, recorded in the former division, was recruited by the support of Rhode Island, New Jersey, Pennsylvania, and Delaware. Had New Hampshire stood by her weaker sisters on this occasion the amendment would have carried, as North Carolina was not then represented in Congress and New York's vote was divided.

Rhode Island and New Jersey both sent objection to the clause "no state shall be deprived of territory for the benefit of the United States," based on the theory that this inhibition might be construed as intending the crown lands, which indeed was the very purpose of the insertion.[9] The legislature of Rhode Island asked for an explanatory addition to the clause to prevent such construction, in these words:

Provided, nevertheless, that all lands within those states, the property of which before the present war was vested in the crown of Great Britain, or out of which revenues from quit-rents arise, payable to the said crown, shall be deemed, taken, and considered, as the property of the United States; and be disposed of and appropriated by Congress, for the benefit of the whole confederacy, reserving, however, to the states within whose limits such crown lands may be, the entire and complete jurisdiction thereof.

The New Jersey objections appear in a Representation of the Legislative Council and General Assembly of that state, an impressive document consisting of a series of remarks arranged in nine numbered paragraphs, each item a criticism of some point in the confederation, with an alteration suggested, and argument supporting the proposed changes. The New Jersey criticisms cover a wide range of ideas, but two of the paragraphs deal with land matters. The first suggests that the boundaries and limits of each state ought to be fully and finally fixed and made known as a means of preventing jealousies and controversies and promoting harmony and confidence among the states. If this could not be done before the proposal of confederation, the principles ought to be established beforehand upon which the determination might be conducted at an early period, not

---

[9] The record of the division in Congress on the motion to adopt the ninth article containing this objectionable clause, taken October 27, 1777, shows the delegate of Rhode Island, Mr. Marchant, casting the vote of his state in the affirmative.

exceeding five years from the final ratification of the confederation. The New Jersey reference to the meaning of "territory" in the prohibitive clause inquires

Whether we are to understand that by territory is intended any land, the property of which was heretofore vested in the crown of Great Britain, or that no mention of such land is made in the confederation, we are constrained to observe, that the present war, as we always apprehended, was undertaken for the general defence and interest of the confederating colonies, now the United States. It was ever the confident expectation of this state, that the benefits derived from a successful contest were to be general and proportionate; and that the property of the common enemy, falling in consequence of a prosperous issue of the war, would belong to the United States, and be appropriated to their use. We are therefore greatly disappointed in finding no provision made in the confederation for empowering the Congress to dispose of such property, but especially the vacant and impatented lands, commonly called the crown lands, for defraying the expenses of the war, and for such other publick and general purposes. The jurisdiction ought in every instance to belong to the respective states within the charter or determined limits of which such lands may be seated; but reason and justice must decide, that the property which existed in the crown of Great Britain, previous to the present revolution, ought now to belong to the Congress, in trust for the use and benefit of the United States. They have fought and bled for it in proportion to their respective abilities; and therefore the reward ought not to be predilectionally distributed. Shall such states as are shut out by situation from availing themselves of the least advantage from this quarter, be left to sink under an enormous debt, while others are enabled, in a short period, to replace all their expenditures from the hard earnings of the whole confederacy?

The dignified form of the New Jersey objections, to say nothing of their serious import, deserved from Congress the most careful consideration of the several points raised against the articles of confederation; but the document, apparently, received even less attention than was accorded to others of much scantier significance. The representation was adopted at Trenton on the 16th of June. It was laid before Congress in the canvas of objections on Tuesday, June 23, and taken into consideration on Thursday. Upon the reading of the paper it was moved "that the several articles in the confederation referred to in the foregoing representation be so far reconsidered as to admit the purport and meaning of the additions, alterations and amendments proposed." There was no discussion of the motion nor of the merits of the separate items. They were not debated seriatim as in the case of other states. The entire set of nine objections was cast out by a single blanket motion to reconsider, on which the record stands: "Question put, Passed in the negative. Three ayes, six noes, one divided."

This rapid manner of disposing of objections brought the congressional canvas of returns from the thirteen states to a close by night of the third session,[10] but the confederation was not concluded with the expedition planned. Not one objection had been sustained. The plan as finished in November was enacted without change in June. All that remained was ratification by subscriptions in Congress to the Act of Confederation at the hands of the authorized delegates of the respective states. Preparations were made speedily for accomplishing this in a ceremonious manner. The 4th of July was approaching, and Congress had ordered adjournment to Philadelphia, where on the sabbath day they were to appear in a body in church, and participate in the celebration planned for the second anniversary of the birth of independence. Confederation might well be concluded on the natal day. But there were slips in the programme. The act of confederation and form of ratification agreed upon were elegantly engrossed

---

[10] There was no confederation business in Congress, Wednesday, June 24.

on a roll of parchment, with spaces ruled in double column for signatures of states in geographical order. The parchment "was laid before congress Saturday, June 27, but the same upon examination being found incorrect, it was ordered that another copy be made, and laid before congress on or before the 4th of July next." In the confusion of adjournment, or for other reason, the day passed without the subscriptions, and the signatures were not called for until the 9th day of July, in the third year of independence.

But these were merely temporary interruptions; the serious difficulty developed at the ceremony of subscription. Eight states ratified the act of confederation, spaces for five state signatures remained vacant on the roll. Delegates of four states waived objections, disregarding specific instructions from their constituency, and signed the engrossment. North Carolina and Georgia, whose legislatures had voted to ratify, did not sign the roll as "they were not at this time represented in congress." When called upon to endorse the parchment as others had done "the delegates from the state of New Jersey, Delaware, and Maryland informed congress that they had not yet received powers to ratify and sign."[11] So the ceremony failed, and confederation was doomed to wait while Congress took measures for persuading the refractory legislatures. A committee was ordered to prepare a circular letter to the backward states, "informing them how many and what states have already ratified, and desiring that they will authorize their delegates to ratify the confederation with all convenient despatch."

The second appeal of congress, issued under date of July 10, 1778, repeats the plea of immediate necessity of confederation, so earnestly employed in the November address. "Influenced by considerations so powerful, and duly weighing the difficulties . . . Congress have, after mature deliberation, agreed to adopt without amendments the confederation transmitted to the several states for their approbation. The states of New Hampshire, Massachusetts Bay, Rhode Island and Providence Plantations, Connecticut, New York, Pennsylvania, Virginia, North Carolina[12] and South Carolina, have ratified the same, and it remains only with your state to conclude the glorious compact . . . . trusting to future deliberations to make such alterations and amendments, as experience may show to be expedient and just."

Two of the remaining states complied with this request, but not without considerable reluctance. New Jersey acted November 20, and Delaware on the 1st of February following. Coupled with the official instructions issued to the delegates of these states were resolutions of the respective legislatures, in almost the same words, disapproving of the articles of confederation " as unequal and disadvantageous to this state;" declaring "the objections lately stated and sent to the general congress are still viewed as just and reasonable, and sundry of them as of the most essential moment to the welfare and happiness of the good people of the state;" and protesting that they ratified "under the full conviction of the present necessity of acceding to the confederacy proposed, and of postponing every separate and detached state interest to the general good of the union, and, moreover, in firm reliance that the candour and justice of the several states, will

[11] The original parchment roll of the engrossed Act of Confederation with signatures, in excellent preservation, is in the Library of the U. S. Department of State, Washington, D. C.
[12] North Carolina is included in this list in the circular letter on the basis of unofficial knowledge, for the record list of signatory states omits North Carolina.

in due time, remove as far as possible, the inequalities which now subsist."

The objections mentioned in the Delaware protest were adopted by the legislature a few days previous to the passage of the powers of ratification. It was then rather late for objections, but Delaware had been slow in dealing with the plan, which was not taken up by the council at Dover until the 3d of December, 1778. At that time the second call for speedy ratification was also in hand. Still there was delay to accommodate the Senate which "was desirous of knowing the sentiments of the people on a subject so materially affecting their interests." Objections were formulated and adopted, and a few days later the resolutions of ratification were passed. Thus there were two sets of resolutions on confederation forwarded as credentials to the delegates of Delaware; first, the objections of January 28, which were directed against the land policy on the same basis as the Maryland objections, and second, the powers for ratification issued to the delegates with the protest of February 1. The presentation of the Delaware credentials caused a stir in Congress. The powers for ratification were lodged with the secretary February 16, 1779, and the roll was signed for Delaware on February 22d. The following day the delegate of Delaware laid before congress the objections to the articles of confederation declaring in favor of absolute national control of the western limits of the claimant states; and national disposition of the extensive tract of country which lies to the westward of the frontier of the United States. On which it was

Resolved, That the paper laid before congress by the delegate of Delaware and read, be filed; provided, that it shall never be considered as admitting any claim by the same set up or intended to be set up.[13]

Meanwhile the signatory states waited with more or less impatience for the disaffected ones to close the circle of confederacy and put an end to the growing embarrassment of congress. The open discord among the states and the uncertainity of their confederating were regarded as the principal cause of the prolonging of the war. Most of the blame for the delay rested on Maryland, but Virginia, whose pretentions had excited the first criticism, did not escape censure. Agitation of the land question gave the Virginians much concern, as the delay in confederating interfered with certain plans of the commonwealth respecting the back lands. Already the Old Dominion had moved to occupy their ultra-montane claims. At this critical moment large grants of lands were being made by the Virginia Assembly to speculators, and wide areas in the disputed territory designated for distribution exclusively to the Virginia soldiery. Whilst the eleventh state was still pondering on this point of union, and without the slightest consideration for the rights of other claimants, Virginia assumed sole possession of everything westward of the Ohio River, and passed an act extending the dominion of the commonwealth, in setting up a sub-administration across the Ohio, to the uncertain limits of the Illinois. Further delay in the Union of states might imperil these ambitious enterprises. The time has come to force the obstructing members to the terms of confederation. Thus conceiving, the Virginia assembly issued instructions to their delegates in Congress to propose a partial confederacy "of so many states as shall be willing." Such a scheme seemed certain to bring in the procrastinators, or it might, perchance, result in the dissolution of the last refractory state,

---

[13] The division on this motion shows New Jersey, Delaware, and Maryland voting together in the negative. Mr. Gouverneur Morris, a delegate of New York, voted no also, but was out-voted by his three colleagues. Later, at critical times, in the land controversy Mr. Morris acted with the minority.

and the possible distribution of the Calvert domain among the abutting colonies. This act passed the assembly, December 18, 1778, but it was not made public in Congress for several months. It was followed, April 7, after Delaware's ratification, by powers issued to the Connecticut delegates to accede to a confederation of twelve states, omitting Maryland. This action also was kept from the records, although known unofficially. Evidently it was the plan to bring these acts into operation at a favorable moment. But Maryland was prepared. Early in December she took action that turned public approval in her favor, shifted the burden of blame to Virginia, and made the first advance towards surrender of the territorial land claim beyond the Ohio.

The fears of Maryland respecting the use that might be made of the vacant land, if the claimant states were not restrained by provisions in the articles of confederation, apply directly to the plans of her neighbor state to seize and hold the whole extent of disputed territory. Virginia laid foundation for the broadest expansion of her dominion, in the beginning, at the moment of transition from the condition of a royal British colony to that of a free American commonwealth, in the assumption of the second charter of King James, issued to the "Virginia" of 1609, as the basis of her rights in America. A number of events in the latter history of the American colonies tend to establish the west boundary line of the claimants' territory at the "sources of the rivers which fall into the Atlantic ocean from the west to the northwest," but Virginia clung to the doctrine of the hinterland as the foundation of her domain, and steadfastly pushed her borders westward; first, over the greater mountains, upon the western waters, and thence across the river to the uttermost reaches of the Illinois, until, in the land cession of 1783, she was forced to drop the prize. The claims in the Virginia constitution, quoted on an earlier page as the initial cause of alarm in the colonies, made the extent of the new-formed commonwealth to stand as fixed in this charter, modified by the more recent limitation of the French Treaty; comprehending

All that space and circuit of land lying from the sea-coast, two hundred miles each way from the Point or Cape Comfort, up into the land throughout from sea to sea [Mississippi River], west and northwest.

Provisions were made in the constitutional paragraph releasing, for prudential reasons, the portions of territory on the eastern waters which were actually covered by her sister colonies, but there were no allowances on the western waters for the claims of other states whose charter limits fall within the area blocked out in the Stuart grant. Virginia had no intention of recognizing the right of any other colony in that direction. It was the latent purpose of Virginia to enter and occupy this reserved domain of the crown, and to have and to hold the soil exclusively until, peopled by her soldiery, "one or more territories, by act of legislature, shall hereafter be laid off, and governments established, westward of the Allegany mountains.[14]"

[14] The assumption of Virginia respecting her chartered limits was never put to proof. The generous concession of a portion of the territory made in 1784 rendered proof of claims unnecessary, and Congress magnanimously accepted the cession on its face value without insisting on proofs of title. Proof was unnecessary also because the United States held by prior and higher claims the Iroquois deed of 1701, and the definitive treaty of 1783. Ex parte statements on the value of the Virginia title have not been lacking from that time to this; the latest is "a communication from the governor of Virginia transmitting certain correspondence and reports in reference to the claims of Virginia against the United States government on account of the cession of

The objection heard in Congress respecting the territorial land claims was general and not particular, and no protest against individual state claims was made until towards the last. Maryland made her objections felt in the matter of controlling the Chesapeake waters by an early conference with Virginia and a joint commission,

to consider of the most proper means to adjust and confirm the right of each, to the use and navigation of, and jurisdiction over the Bay of Chesapeake, and the rivers Potomac and Pocomoke.

But no state made local challenge of the proposed rule of the commonwealth of Virginia on the western waters.

The first mark of the purpose of Virginia to occupy the back country is in the prohibitive clause appendant to the description of the charter limits of the commonwealth enacted May 6, 1776:

No purchase of lands shall be made of the Indian nations, but in behalf of the public, by authority of the general assembly.

It was the well established policy of the British crown and colonies that the title of an Indian was not in itself sufficient to convey the right of property,[15] but occasion called for the early application of this principle in Virginia, with respect to the disputed lands, while the convention was still in session, in the following form:

Whereas, divers petitions from the inhabitants on the western frontiers have been presented to this convention, complaining of exorbitant demands made on them for lands claimed by persons pretending to derive title from Indian deeds and purchases.
Resolved, That all persons actually settled on any of the said lands ought to hold the same, without paying any pecuniary or other consideration whatever to any private person or persons, until the said petitions, as well as the validity of the titles under such Indian deeds and purchases, shall have been considered and determined on by the legislature of this country; and that all persons who are now actually settled on any unlocated or unappropriated lands in Virginia, to which there is no other just claim, shall have the pre-emption or preference, in the grant of such lands.
Resolved, That no purchases of lands within the chartered limits of Virginia, shall be made, under any pretense whatever, from any Indian tribe or nation, without the approbation of the Virginia legislature.

The petitioners referred to in these resolutions are "inhabitants of that part of America called Transylvania," from whom one petition is recorded in the Journal of the Convention under date of May 18. They complain of the unjust and arbitrary proceedings of Richard Henderson and Company, the proprietors of that country in which the petitioners had made settlements under expectation of undoubted title. They doubt the validity of the purchase those proprietors have made of the Cherokees, "the only title they set up to the lands for which they demand such exorbitant sums of money," as it was in conflict with a deed which they had lately seen, executed at Fort Stanwix, in which the confederated Indians of the Six Nations "declared the Cherokee [Tennessee] river to be their true boundary with the southward Indians." As they had purchased from the Henderson

---

the Northwest Territory" (Va. Sen. Doc. No. III, Jan. 24, 1910), wherein it is proposed to the legislature that a demand shall be made upon the United States for a refund of a share of $119,479,204 due Virginia as reserve interest in ceded lands misappropriated by the United States for education, public improvement, and other local benefits.

[15] Chief Justice Marshall ruled "that a title to lands derived solely from a grant made by an Indian tribe northwest of the Ohio in 1773 and 1775 to private individuals cannot be recognized in the courts of the United States" (8 Wharton, p. 543).

Company they asked for relief from the convention of Virginia, or an espousal of their claim in Congress as the cause of the colony.

The proprietors of the Transylvania purchase answered these petitions in a memorial which appears at great length in the convention proceedings of June 15, in which they seek to clear themselves of the heavy charges of injustice, exorbitant, and arbitrary measures. They deny also certain insinuations "of setting themselves up as absolute proprietors of an independent province; and of attempting to dismember the colony by sending delegates or a memorial to Congress." They claim also priority of title to the convention and the commonwealth of Virginia, arguing that a declaration of independence cannot alter the tenure of estates, or a change of government interfere with the rights of private individuals to hold property; and they demand a hearing of the matters charged in the petitions.[16]

The petitions and the memorial were in the hands of committees of the convention, and they passed over as impending business to corresponding committees of the general assembly when that body was organized under the commonwealth. The references to attempts to set up independent governments at different locations along the Ohio were transmitted to the delegates in Congress to forestall action there. The Henderson case called for an inquiry into the nature of the Iroquois claims to the Cherokee country, and commissions were assigned to take depositions of the Indian chiefs at Williamsburg and in the Washington district. Thus matters stood in the middle of the second session of the Virginia assembly when, on the 3d of June, 1777, a memorial appeared from the proprietors of a tract of land on the Ohio, called Indiana.

The memorial of the Indiana Company, known in after proceedings in the land controversy in the Continental Congress, raised the direct point with the commonwealth of the right of title of the Six United Nations to practically all of the back country from the Wisconsin to the central ridges of the Alleghanies, upon which the claims of the New York colony had rested for almost a century. The memorialists claimed property as conveyed by the Six United Nations at a treaty held at Fort Stanwix in the year 1768, setting forth

"That the grant was obtained of the grantors under the immediate superintendence of Sir William Johnson, and executed in the presence of the Governor

---

[16] Other petitions of this nature are found running through the printed records of the final session of the convention of Virginia, and the succeeding sessions of the general assembly, and elsewhere in the published archives of Virginia. They tell the same story

. . . of the hardships that would result to the petitioners and others, from grants of large tracts of lands to private companies of gentlemen, which were to be sold out at a moderate price for the encouragement and speedy settlement of the back country, but that agents to the company and their successors, instead of adhering to their first proposals, have demanded, and actually received enormous prices, and have, by various unfair practices, either sold, located or claimed nearly double their first grant.

Certain petitioners set forth that they had

. . . entered on the lands they occupied many years before and cultivated them with great labor and expense, often at the peril of their lives from savages, in consequence of which they hoped they had obtained a just and equitable title to their possessions, without being obliged to contribute large sums of money for the separate emolument of individuals whose mercenary views are incompatible with the real good of the community.

Petitions are recorded also from companies holding grants to take up and survey lands issued "by the governor and council under the former British government." The purchasers had made investments in explorations and surveys, in roadways and other improvements, and they had sold off much of their lands to actual settlers, but their contracts were impaired and their operations interrupted by the general feeling of unrest in the colonies, and by the uncertainty regarding titles, and all would be lost unless the titles were confirmed.

of New Jersey, and others, among whom were the commissioners then attending in behalf of the colony of Virginia."

They conceive that by the convention resolve of the 24th of June last,

Virginia had laid a foundation for calling in question the title of the memorialists to the lands aforesaid; if the title of the memorialists should be called into discussion, conscious of the equity and validity of their right, they shall never hesitate to submit it to a proper judicature, nor to defend it in the ordinary course of justice; that, under these circumstances, they confide the legislature of Virginia will not, by any act or proceeding whatever, impeach or prejudice their title, so well established, on the principles of reason, equity, and sound policy.

The memorial, when read, was referred to the committee of the whole house upon the state of the commonwealth, the same committee that had charge of the Henderson case. The matter dragged along through the third session, during which the Henderson case was appointed to a hearing and postponed. It must not be supposed that the Virginia general assembly mistook the gravity of the situation. On the last day of the third session action came of a significant character. The record for January 24, 1778, reads:

"The clerk of the house was ordered to transmit a copy of the several papers filed in the office relating to the claim of Richard Henderson and Company and the Indiana Company, to George Mason and Thomas Jefferson, Esquires."

This was done, no doubt, to fortify the assembly with opinions; and on the same day these resolutions were agreed to:

Whereas, it is of the greatest importance to this commonwealth, that the waste and unappropriated lands to which no person having just claim should be disposed of, for the purpose of creating a sinking fund, in aid of the taxes for discharging the public debt, and to the end that the claims to unpatented lands, under the former or present government, may not in the meantime be increased or strengthened.

Resolved, that every entry, with the survey hereafter made in the country upon the western waters under any pretense or title whatsoever, until the land office shall be established and the manner and terms of granting waste and unappropriated lands, shall be void and of no effect; and that no persons hereafter settling in the country upon the said western waters, shall be entitled to any land or pre-emption of land for such settlement, without paying for the same such consideration as shall be hereafter ascertained by the general assembly, so as no family be entitled to more than 400 acres.

Resolved, That all persons claiming any unpatented lands on the said western waters by order of council, shall lay the same before the general assembly on or before the 20th day of their next session, and be at liberty in the mean time to take the depositions of any witnesses they may choose, to examine such claims, giving reasonable notice thereof to the person appointed by the governor and council to attend such examination in the county, on behalf of the commonwealth, in case such person shall be appointed.

Finally, after two years, the Henderson case was heard in the Virginia assembly. The hearing was conducted with dignity, with "the Senate invited to take seats in the House, while the memorials and papers were read and arguments heard at the bar." Richard Henderson, chief promotor of Transylvania, appeared in person. He asked for a separate court of judicature, and proposed as the issue the simple question "whether the title obtained by the claimants from the Cherokees was sufficient to convey the right of property." They argued for the justice of the Cherokee claim as against the claim of the Six United Nations, citing the constant and perpetual occupancy by the Cherokees and the recognition by the Virginia colonial government in treaties and purchases made of the Cherokee nation.[17] Conclusion was reached in the case November 4, 1778. The Henderson purchase was declared void, and the doctrine of invalidity of Indian titles reaffirmed in this form:

Resolved, That all purchases of lands made or to be made of the Indians within the chartered boundaries of this commonwealth, as described by the constitution and form of Government, by any private person not authorized by public authority is void.

Compensation was to be allowed to the claimants " for their great expense in making the purchases and in settling the lands, by which this commonwealth are very like to receive great advantage, by increasing its inhabitants and establishing a barrier against the Indians"; and a commission was ordered, to consider "what compensation it may be just and reasonable to allow for the service rendered this commonwealth in quieting the minds of the Cherokee Indians, and in settling many families upon that tract of land in the back country, commonly called Transylvania."

The way was now clear for the inquiry called for in the memorial of the Indiana Company. A day was set in the May session for a hearing, and public notice was inserted in the *Virginia Gazette* for all concerned to attend. Meanwhile petitions and memorials were accumulating, and the minutes of the assembly were burdened with applications for confirmation of titles obtained in various ways: lands taken up for homesteads, purchases from the Indians, grants of the Dunmore government, army warrants, under the royal proclamation, or under orders of the governor and council. The claims antedate the Virginia constitution, but they are all illegal under the retroactive aspect of the constitution. They must be swept out of the chartered territory of Virginia and all unpatented lands reclaimed, from the boundaries of Pennsylvania southwest to the indeterminate lines of the Carolinas and Georgia. The finding of the Indiana Company case, after a ceremonious hearing June 9, 1779, marks the climax of activity in these expulsions:

Resolved, That the commonwealth of Virginia hath the exclusive right of pre-emption, from the Indians, of all lands within the limits of its own chartered territory, as declared by the act and constitution or form of government in 1776, that no person or persons whatsoever have, or ever had, a right to purchase any land within the same from any Indian nation, except only persons duly authorized to make such purchases on the public account, formerly for the use and benefit of the colony, and lately of the commonwealth; and that such exclusive right or pre-emption will, and ought to be, maintained by this commonwealth to the utmost of its power.

Resolved, That every purchase of land heretofore made by the King of Great Britain from any Indian nation or nations, within the before mentioned limits, doth and ought to enure forever to and for the use and benefit of this commonwealth, and to and for no other use or purpose whatsoever.

Resolved, Therefore, That the deed from the six united nations of Indians, bearing date on the third day of November, 1768, for certain lands between the Alleghany mountains and the river Ohio, above the mouth of the little Kanawha creek, to and for the use and benefit of a certain William Trent, gentleman, in his own right, and as attorney for sundry persons in the said deed named, as well as all other deeds which have been or shall be made by any Indian or Indians, or by an Indian nation or nations, for lands within the limits of the charter and territory of Virginia as aforesaid, to or for the use or benefit of any private person or persons, shall be, and the same are hereby declared utterly void, and of no effect.

[17] A second Henderson memorial is recorded Oct. 29, 1778, in the House journal. Final agreement, November 30, allows 400,000 acres on Green River to Henderson and Co.

In order to remove and prevent all doubt concerning purchases of land from the Indian nations, the general assembly framed the first and second resolution into a bill and enacted the same on the 17th of June at this session, with the title: An act for declaring and asserting the rights of this commonwealth, concerning purchasing land from Indian nations.[18]

While the general assembly was thus striving to establish a jurisdiction over the disputed territory, and to set up a revenue for the benefit of the public exigencies by wholesale reclamations of the soil of the back lands, the Old Dominion unexpectedly gained the chance to expand the government of the commonwealth over the entire area of her claims. Clark had heard the call of conquest in the wilds of Kentucky, and hurrying to the capital secured a commission of secret invasion. He mustered his militiamen in Virginia for an overland crusade to Detroit, and having crossed the Ohio halted at the Kaskaskies, with the result well known to fame. Clark brought as his trophy to the commonwealth a fictitious estate for an empty treasury. When lands were lacking in every colony to satisfy overwhelming requirements of bounty obligations, he opened a way for Virginia to the fabulous wealth of an immeasurable wilderness. All other land claims were as nothing compared with these, and Virginia had secured all. These delusive prospects of profit in the sales of Ohio lands lay in the marvellous fertility of the soil, in the abundance of natural products, in salt springs known to abound, and in traditional mineral deposits of gold, silver, copper, and lead along the river. Here was land for ready sale, an imaginary asset, sufficient to indemnify Virginia for all the past expenditures of war, to pay off all bounty promises, to furnish a means for permanent reduction of taxation, and to leave vast areas untouched for future uses.

Virginia lost no time in securing this new property. It is recorded under date of the 19th of November, 1778, that "the speaker laid before the House, a letter from the governor, enclosing several letters and papers from Lieut. Col. Clarke and Captain Leonard Helm." The letters and papers, being read, were referred to a committee named, to whom leave was given to prepare and bring in a bill "for establishing a county, to include the inhabitants of this commonwealth, on the western side of the Ohio river, and for the better government of those inhabitants." This is the record of the act to establish the county of Illinois, the land of Clark's triumph, and to provide a temporary form of government adapted to the circumstances of the new citizens of the commonwealth, French and Canadians, who had taken the oath of fidelity to Virginia "on the westward side of the Ohio, in the vicinity of the Mississippi." No other description is necessary! The legal bounds of the new county embrace all that remains of the expanse of the King James charter, up into the land throughout, "from sea to river, west and northwest" from Old Point Comfort.[19]

It was in this session of the general assembly, in which it was ordained to establish this distant dependency of the commonwealth on territory claimed by sister states and on lands still in controversy in the general congress, and while the tenure of land cases were actually depending on the

[18] Hening's Statutes, vol. 10, p. 97.
[19] The indefinite limits of the county of Illinois as expressed in the act, although actually including the entire northwest, must be understood to mean the limited region defined by Thomas Hutchins in his topographical description of Virginia, issued in 1778, as "that part of my Map called Illinois Country, lying between the Mississippi westerly, the Illinois River northerly, the Wabash easterly, and the Ohio southerly." The act is in Hening's Statutes, vol. 9, p. 553.

decision of the assembly, that the Virginia house of delegates developed the plan of forcing immediate conclusion of the confederacy. The bill creating the county of Illinois became a law on the 30th of December, 1778. On the same day the plan was formulated in the house to bring the backward states quickly to the terms of a confederation so favorable to Virginia's hopes. The matter was under consideration until the 18th, when the house came to the following resolutions, which the next day were concurred in by the Senate :

Resolved, nemine contra dicente, That our delegates in Congress be instructed to propose to Congress, that they recommend to each of the states named as parties in the articles of confederation, heretofore laid before and ratified by the assembly, that they authorize their delegates in Congress to ratify the said articles, together with the delegates of so many other of the said states, as shall be willing, so that the same shall be forever binding on the states so ratifying, notwithstanding that a part of those named shall decline to ratify the same; allowing, nevertheless, to the said states so declining, either a given or an indefinite time, as to Congress shall seem best, for acceding to the said confedereration, and making themselves thereby members of the Union.

Resolved, nemine contra dicente, That our said delegates now in office, or hereafter to be appointed, be authorized and required, and they are hereby authorized and required to ratify the said articles of confederation on the part of this commonwealth, with so many of the other states, named in them as parties, as shall on their part ratify the same.

Resolved, nemine contra dicente, That it be an instruction to the Virginia delegates, to inform Congress of the resolutions of this general assembly, respecting purchases of lands from any Indian nation.

Entered next after this in the journal, in a form indicating that they are part of a single connected action, are these items :

And whereas the assembly hath come to believe that sundry citizens of some of the United States, were, and are, connected and concerned with some of the King of Great Britain's late governors in America, as well as with sundry noblemen and others, subjects of the said King, in the purchase of a very large tract of land from the Indians, on the northwest side of the Ohio river, within the territory of Virginia,

Resolved, Also, That the said delegates be instructed to use their endeavors in Congress, to cause an inquiry to be made, concerning the said purchase, and whether any, and what citizens of any of the United States, were, or are, concerned therein.

The more effectually to enable Congress to comply with the promise of a bounty in lands to the officers and soldiers of the army, on continental establishment;

Resolved, That this commonwealth will, in conjunction with such other of the United States as have unappropriated back lands, furnish out of its territory, between the rivers Ohio and Mississippi, in such proportion as shall hereafter be adjusted and settled by Congress, its proper quota or proportion of such lands, without any purchase money, to the troops on continental establishment of such of the United States, as already have acceded, or shall within such time, given or indefinite, as to Congress shall seem best, accede to the confederation of the United States, and who have not within their own respective territory, unappropriated lands for that purpose; and that a copy of this resolve, be forthwith transmitted to the Virginia delegates, to be by them communicated to Congress.

Not all of this volley of resolutions of the Virginia assembly reached the intended mark, as some of the items have not been located in the journals or papers of the Continental Congress ; and not one of them produced the results desired. The edict of the commonwealth against Indian grants would serve as a "no trespass" notice to all the states until a land office route to the preserves was open. The warning of a British invasion by colonization fell short of the general congress. The proffer of land from her own abundance, for the bounty dues of landless states, seems like a a reward of merit for good behavior. It was read in Congress on the 26th of January and repeated, with protestations of sincerity, in the first land session proposition of 1781. The lands intended for this generosity were in Ohio territory; but as the lands were still claimed by New York and Connecticut, and as the general controversy respecting their ultimate disposition was still pending in Congress, the offer to distribute them to pay off the debts of a few states could not well be entertained in that body. The main resolution proposing confederation without Maryland did not reach the files of Congress at once. Doubtless it found the popular channel of publicity of that day, being privately printed as "broadsides" and distributed with signatures attached. It cannot be said that it influenced the action of Delaware, and its effect on Maryland was not quite what was expected by the authors of the resolution. One response may or may not be attributed to it: the issue at Hartford on the 7th of April of power to the Connecticut delegates to conclude confederation without the thirteenth state.

But Maryland had made ready for the assault. Fully anticipating the responsibility that must come upon the state as last obstinate objector in the confederation dispute, the general assembly had prepared a justification of past action and had taken counsel of the sense and deliberate judgment of the state for a future course. It was decided that the state should remain independent, continuing in loyalty to the original compact of colonies until liberty was won, but not confederating on the basis proposed.

The declaration of intentions respecting confederation, and the personal instructions to their six delegates in Congress for use of the same, were prepared by the Maryland assembly simultaneously with the Virginia series of resolves. The two instruments bear date of December 15, four days ahead of the Virginia proposition. The Maryland declaration is a restatement of the series of resolves, remonstrance, and instructions[20] of the assembly in the course of the dispute, upon which the amendments and alterations proposed on behalf of the State from time to time were drawn, while the second instrument conveys assurances to the delegates of the sentiments of the state, and explicit directions for their final action on confederation.

The declaration of Maryland was laid before Congress by the delegates of that state on Wednesday, January 6, 1779, but it was not then considered. It is not recorded as read in Congress, nor does it appear anywhere in the journals,[21] but it is not to be doubted that the sentiments it expressed respecting the confederacy were "made publicly known and explicitly and concisely declared," since the delegates were directed in the instructions

.... to have it printed and to present signed copies thereof to each of the delegates of other states to the intent and purpose that copies may be communi-

---

[20] The instructions here referred to are in the action of the Maryland general assembly of the previous June, which had formed the basis of objections urged in Congress against confederation at that time:
Resolved, That the delegates from this state consider themselves bound by the instructions given in October session last, and that they endeavour to procure from Congress an explicit answer to the propositions therein contained; but that they do not at any time consider themselves at liberty to ratify or confirm any confederation of perpetual friendship and union, until they have communicated such answer to the general assembly of this state and shall receive their express authority to do so.
[21] It is stated in the final act of ratification of the Maryland Assembly, adopted February 2, 1781, and read in Congress February 12, that the declaration "stands entered on the journals of Congress," but no such endorsement appears on the original ms. document, which is in the papers of the Continental Congress, No. 70, p. 293.

cated to our brethren in the United States, and the contents taken into their serious and candid consideration.

The old argument appears in the declaration of the injustice and unfairness in the exclusive use of the crown lands by individual states, but additional force and effect is secured by reference to certain preparations for immediate sales of the vacant lands. However, the most interesting feature of the paper is the fresh cry of alarm raised on account of newly discovered dangers in the proposed confederation.

Maryland apprehensions were aroused by the reading of Article III of the confederation, which seems to be merely an expression in fervent language of the "firm bond of friendship" which was to hold the sister states in perpetual amity. By this bond the assembly seemed to fear that Maryland might be "burthened with heavy expenses for the subduing and guaranteeing immense tracts of country, although having no share of the moneys arising from the sales of the lands within those tracts or be otherwise benefitted thereby." It is stated:

> We declare that we mean not to subject ourselves to such guaranty nor will we be responsible for any part of such expense, unless the third article and proviso [of article IX] be explained so as to prevent their being hereafter construed in a manner injurious to this state.[22]

There are promises, also, that Maryland will accede to the confederation provided the desired amendments are made,

> expressly reserving or securing to the United States a right in common in, and to all the lands lying to the westward of the frontiers as aforesaid, not granted to, surveyed for, or purchased by individuals at the commencement of the present war, in such manner that the said lands be sold out, or otherwise disposed of for the common benefit of all the states; and that the money arising from the sale of those lands, or the quit rents reserved thereon, may be deemed and taken as part of the moneys belonging to the United States, and as such be appropriated by Congress towards defraying the expenses of the war, and the payment of interest on moneys borrowed or to be borrowed on the credit of the United States from France or any other European power, or for any other joint benefit of the United States.

The final paragraph of the declaration pledges Maryland's adherence to the cause of freedom until independence is firmly established, but shifts the responsibility for prolongation of the war upon those "who by refusing to comply with requisitions so just and reasonable have hitherto prevented the confederation from taking place, and are therefore justly chargeable with every evil which have flowed and may flow from such procrastination."[23]

No trace of the instructions appears in the January record of Congress. This document was not filed with the declaration, but was read in secret and held in reserve by the Maryland delegation to answer the call for further powers for ratification, should that be heard. The paper instructs the delegates respecting the use of the declaration, and directs them as to the votes they give and the opinions they deliver in Congress respecting confederation. "We have spoken with freedom as becomes freemen, and we sincerely wish that our representations, may make such an impression on that assembly as to induce them to make such addition to the articles of confederation as may bring about a permanent union."

[22] Article III of the confederation reads as follows:
The said states hereby severally enter into a firm league of friendship with each other, for their common defence, the security of their liberties, and their mutual and general welfare; binding themselves to assist each other, against all force offered to, or attacks made upon them, or any of them on account of religion, sovereignty, trade or any other pretence whatever.
[23] Printed in full in Hening's Statutes, vol. 10, p. 549.

Maryland's course of opposition is explained at length, and the obstruction of the confederation is fully justified to the delegates on patriotic grounds. The private use of the crown lands, which were secured at common expense, is the main point. The instability of the proposed union, formed on so great an injustice, is argued on the theory that the states which have acceded to the present confederation contrary to their own interests and judgments will consider it no longer binding when the causes cease to operate, and will eagerly embrace the first occasion of asserting their just rights and securing their independence. The preparations of Virginia to sell the lands is cited as to what may be expected.

Suppose Virginia indisputably possessed of the extensive and fertile country to which she has set up a claim, what would be the consequences to Maryland? They cannot escape the least discerning. Virginia, by selling on the most moderate terms a small portion of the lands in question would draw into her treasury vast sums of money, and in proportion to the sums arising from such sales would be enabled to lessen her taxes. Lands comparatively cheap and taxes comparatively low with the lands and taxes of an adjacent state, would quickly drain the state thus disadvantageously circumstanced of its most useful inhabitants, its wealth, and its consequence in the scale of confederated states would sink of course.

The declared intention of Virginia to relinquish at some future period a portion of the country contended for is criticised " as made to lull suspicion asleep, and to cover the design of a secret ambition ; or, if the thought were seriously entertained, the lands are now claimed to reap an immediate profit from the sales." The argument of nationalizing the crown lands follows, and then the words :

We have coolly and dispassionately considered the subject; we have weighed probable inconveniences and hardships against the sacrifice of just and essential rights; and do instruct you not to agree to the confederation unless an article or articles be added thereto in conformity with our declaration. Should we succeed in obtaining such article or articles, then you are hereby fully empowered to accede to the confederation.[24]

For reasons not disclosed in official records the Virginia resolutions proposing a confederacy of part of the states were not presented in Congress until the 20th of May. On that day the delegates of Virginia laid before Congress an attested copy of the two resolutions of the assembly pertaining to this subject, which had been in their care since the December previous, and the same were read and entered in the journals. In pursuance of the powers and instructions therein contained the delegates moved to carry the resolutions into immediate effect by recommending ratification on the basis proposed, on a fixed date to be determined in Congress. The delegates of Virginia then delivered a paper signed by them in the following words :

In consequence of the foregoing instructions and powers to us given we do hereby declare, that we are ready and willing to ratify the confederation with any one or more states named therein, so that the same shall be forever binding upon the state of Virginia.

    Merewether Smith, Richard Henry Lee.
    Cyrus Griffin,   William Fleming.

No action of Congress is recorded on the Virginia proposition. No discussion took place and, apparently, the motion of the Virginia delegates was not put to vote. The next day's business began with the delegates of

---

[24] The original ms. Instructions are in the papers of the Continental Congress, No. 70, p. 305. The paper is recorded in the journals of Congress under date of May 21, 1779, and may be found in Hening's Statutes, vol. 10, p. 553.

Maryand "informing Congress, that they had received instructions respecting the articles of confederation, which they were directed to lay before Congress, and to have entered on their journals." The Maryland instructions were read by the secretary and were spread upon the pages of the journal. Following this the Connecticut delegation filed the further powers issued to them authorizing them to ratify the confederation with eleven states, omitting Maryland, "in the most full and ample manner. Always provided, that the state of Maryland be not thereby excluded from acceding to said confederation at anytime thereafter."

Confident in the security of her claims from local interference, and no longer fearing the interposition of Congress, the Virginia assembly now made haste with the legislation necessary for immediate disposition of the property to the best advantage of the commonwealth. The long deferred land office was provided for in a bill enacted soon after the close of the Indiana Company hearing. A second bill "for adjusting and settling the titles of claimers to unpatented lands under the present and former governments, previous to the establishment of the commonwealth's land office," was enacted at the same time to ease the anxiety in the settlements on the frontiers.

The land office was to open in October, the terms and manner of granting waste and unappropiated lands were fixed, and a register was appointed to take office immediately. A special order for record books of sales was made in the assembly so that no time would be lost in the remote counties of Monongahela, Yohogania, Ohio, and Kentucky, bordering upon the river. The lands were to be distributed according to the ancient custom to prospectors making entry and survey by county surveyors commissioned by the College of William and Mary, and warrants issued on proof. Officers and soldiers had the preference, as provided by the several bounty laws, and actual settlers on uncontested claims were also privileged to purchase the lands they occupied. All other waste and unappropriated lands on the eastern or western waters, within the territory of the commonwealth, were for sale to any person in quantity desired at the rate of forty pounds per hundred acres. The laws were printed and distributed to the various counties, and extraordinary means were employed to spread abroad quickly the news of the opening of the land office. On the last day of the summer session of the Virginia assembly it was

Resolved, That the Governor be desired to transmit by the post one hundred copies of the act . . . . to the Virginia delegates in Congress, and desire them to take the most speedy and effectual measures for dispensing and publishing the same in the different states.[25]

These laws were intended to apply, until further orders of the Virginia assembly, to lands only as far westward as the Ohio River, but it will not be doubted that it was the plan to extend as soon as practicable to the regions across the river. But the time never came for Virginia to sell off Ohio lands. Disapproval of the land office act arose to prevent it. These laws made actual trespassers of the speculators and settlers along the river, most of whom held title from the confederated Indians. As this was an issue of national magnitude the dispossessed memorialists took an appeal to Congress and secured the interposition of the United States to restrain Virginia.[26]

[25] The acts were passed on the 23d of June. They may be found in Hening's Statutes, vol. 10, pp. 35-65.

[26] George Crogan appeared on the 5th of June before the Virginia House of Dele-

The memorials were presented and read in Congress on the 14th of September. George Morgan, petitioning for the Indiana Company, contends

"that the tract of country claimed by the Indiana Company was separated by the King of Great Britain, before independence was declared, from the dominion, which, in the right of the crown, Virginia claimed over it, and cannot remain subject to the jurisdiction of Virginia, or any particular state, but of the whole United States in Congress, assembled."

Morgan prays for an order to stay Virginia in the sale of the land in question till the case can be heard in Congress, and "the whole rights of the owners of the tract of land called Vandalia, of which Indiana is a part, shall be ascertained in such a manner as may tend to support the sovereignty of the United States and the just rights of the individual therein." The same point was raised by William Trent in a second memorial in regard to the larger tract called Vandalia, and there were other appeals of minor importance.[27]

The delegates of Virginia made instant objection to the consideration of these Papers in Congress, raising for the first time in American politics an issue of state rights. The matter of Virginia's protest does not appear in the records, but from subsequent proceedings in Congress its purport may be known. The objections were based on the doctrine that Congress had no jurisdiction over the subject-matter of the Morgan memorial since it was related to the internal affairs of a sovereign state. The question was put to vote and the reference was ordered. The committee of five delegates elected by vote of states was directed by order of Congress

to enquire into the foundation of the objection formerly made by the Virginia delegates, upon the reading of the petition and the memorial, to the jurisdiction of Congress on the subject matter of the said papers, and first report the facts relating to that point.[28]

The committee took quick action on the protest, with results detrimental to Virginia, declaring

... that they have read over and considered the state of facts given in by the delegates of Virginia, and cannot find any such distinction between the question of jurisdiction of Congress, and the merits of the cause, as to recommend any decision upon the first separately from the last.

And in addition to this, they offer a preamble and a resolution reprobating the action of the commonwealth in opening a land office.

The delegates were in conflict in Congress for two days over this report. There was apparently no trouble in the decision on the point of jurisdiction, for the members seemed to agree with the committee; but on the wording of the preamble, and the substance of the resolution, there were several divisions. Maryland delegates offered a substitute of more drastic criticism of Virginia's land office programme. On this there was a sharp conflict.[29]

---

gates praying to be heard, and on the 9th presented a memorial praying for confirmation of title to three tracts of land on the Ohio purchased in 1749 from the Six Nations. After the decision against the Indiana Company Crogan took his case direct to Congress. Many papers relating to Western claims may be found in the Papers of the Continental Congress, No. 30.

[27] The Morgan memorial is spread on the minutes of Congress. The original Trent memorial is in the papers of the Continental Congress, No. 41, vol. x, p. 79.

[28] The vote was six to five. Connecticut for the first time voted with the non-claimants, New York was divided, and Georgia was not represented.

[29] Mr. Paca of Maryland wished to censure Virginia for opening the land office, because it "has produced much uneasiness, dispute and controversy, and greatly weak-

The Maryland form carried at first, but on reconsideration a more reasonable resolution was adopted, in these words:

Whereas the appropriation of vacant lands by the several states during the continuance of the war, will, in the opinion of Congress, be attended with great mischiefs; therefore,

Resolved, that it be earnestly recommended to the state of Virginia, to reconsider their late act of assembly for opening their land office; and that it be recommended to the said state, and all other states similarly circumstanced, to forbear settling or issuing warrants for unappropriated lands, or granting the same during the continuance of the present war.

Report of this action first reached the Virginia assembly in a letter from the delegates of the commonwealth. The letter and proceedings were read in the house of delegates on the 13th of November and referred to a committee of the whole house on the state of the commonwealth. The committee took up the matter the same day and soon came to resolutions which were at once reported; and, all formalities being suspended in view of the importance of the subject, the resolutions were unanimously agreed to by both house and senate.

Resolved, nemine contra dicente, That a remonstrance be drawn up to the Hon. the American Congress, firmly asserting the right of this commonwealth to its own territory, complaining of their having received petitions from certain persons, styling themselves the Indiana and Vandalia companies, upon claims which not only interfere with the laws and internal policy, but tend to subvert the government of this commonwealth, and introduce general confusion; and expressly excepting and protesting against the jurisdiction of Congress therein as unwarranted by the fundamental principles of the confederation.

Resolved, nemine contra dicente, That the Governor, with the advice of the council, be empowered and required to use the most effectual means for apprehending and securing any person or persons within this commonwealth, who shall attempt to subvert the government thereof, or set up any separate government within the same, that such person or persons may be brought to trial, according to due course of law.

A remonstrance to Congress was issued by Virginia in pursuance of this action, but not in the belligerent tones of the resolutions. The remonstrance bears date of its adoption in the assembly thirty days after the passage of the resolutions. It doubtless found its way directly to the congressional committee, which was still at work on the memorials. The remonstrance assures Congress that, "Although the general assembly of Virginia would make great sacrifices to the common interests of America . . . . and be ready to listen to any just and reasonable propositions for removing the *ostensible* causes of the delay to the complete ratification of the confederation, they . . . . expressly protest against any jurisdiction or right of adjudication in Congress, upon . . . . any matter or thing subversive of the internal policy, civil government, or sovereignty of this or any other of the United American States." There are other interesting features of the remonstrance not anticipated in the resolutions: a warning against establishing dangerous precedents in seizing lands of states; a reminder of the effect of congressional interposition, upon the pending negotiations for peace, in which the charters of the states were to be urged as the basis of definition of the United States boundaries;[30] and a reference to the safety clause in the ninth article of the confederation by which "the rights of sovereignty

---

ened these United States by the emigration of their inhabitants to parts remote from defence against the common enemy." But as the land office had been open less than a month this language was scarcely justifiable.

[30] Cf. Note 6, *supra*.

and jurisdiction within her own territory were reserved and secured to Virginia when she acceded to the articles of confederation." There is information, also, of the offer of the general assembly of bounty lands "out of their territory on the northwest side of the Ohio river," and Congress is assured that "the offer when accepted will be most cheerfully made good." No word appears respecting reconsideration of the land office act, nor of a suspension of the distribution of the vacant lands; but in the first paragraph of the document it is announced that "the general assembly have enacted a law to prevent present settlement on the northwest side of the Ohio river."

The law to prevent present settlements on the northwest side of the Ohio River, referred to in the Virginia remonstrance, is easily identified as a paragraph inserted by the Virginia House as an amendment to a bill relating to the location of warrants on the military reservation, then in its final passage in the assembly. The circumstances of this enactment are interesting. Information was received in the House on the 8th of November, in a communication from the Governor, respecting "intrusions on Indian lands upon the Ohio." From reports[31] received the same day in Congress it is learned that these intruders are

... some of the inhabitants from Yoghiagania and Ohio counties, Virginia, who had crossed the Ohio River and made small improvements on the Indian's lands, from the river Muskingum to Fort McIntosh, and 30 miles up the branches of the Ohio River.

The trespassers had been apprehended and their huts destroyed by the Continentals under Col. Broadhead. In consequence of this news from the frontiers the assembly made haste to enlarge the scope of the pending bill, adding the paragraph prohibiting settlements on the northwest side of the Ohio, and

... desiring the Governor to issue a proclamation, requiring all persons settled on the said land immediately to remove therefrom, and forbidding others to settle in future, and moreover, with the advice of the council from time to time, to order such armed force as shall be thought necessary to remove from the said lands, such person or persons as shall remain on or settle contrary to the said proclamation.[32]

New York, moved by this display of national spirit in Congress, made an immediate surrender of all claims upon the western country. The firm stand of Congress against Virginia, proudest of the claimants, inspired the legislature to relinquish the long standing rights of the state to the Iroquois lands. New York gave up this great property freely, with no thought of reservation, and without suggestion of personal indemnity for the expenses of a century of support of the historic contract with the Six United Nations, from whom the state derived title. The New York cession of territory is in the form of "an act to facilitate the completion of the articles of confederation and perpetual union among the American States," passed by the legislature on the 19th of February, 1780. The act confers full power and authority upon their delegates in Congress,

[31] In a letter of the 26th of October from Col. Broadhead to the president of Congress, on the basis of which Congress ordered a letter enclosing a copy of the letter of Col. Broadhead sent to the Governor of Virginia, from whose jurisdiction the offenders came, "requesting his excellency to endeavor to prevent a repetition of the trespass mentioned in it."

[32] This act is printed in Hening's Statutes, vol. 10, p. 159, but there is no trace of the proclamation.

... to limit and restrict the boundaries of the state in the western parts thereof, either with respect to the jurisdiction or right of pre-emption of soil, or both, and to relinquish the territory to the north and westward of these boundaries, "to be and enure for the use and benefit of such of the United States as shall become members of the federal union."

The New York act of cession was read in Congress on the 7th of March following its passage, and was referred to a committee of three delegates chosen by a vote of the states to consider the matter. The New York act and the unfinished business of the former committee of five, the Maryland and Virginia papers, and the memorials of the Indian claimants, were reported upon six months later, and the famous recommendations of September 6, calling upon the claimant states to surrender a portion of their claims for the general good, is the report of this committee.[33]

Congress took the report into consideration on that date, and it was agreed to as reported. This document is often printed in full in accounts of the land cessions. The committee conceived it to be unnecessary to take up the matters raised in the papers of Maryland and Virginia. They declared

That it appears more advisable to press upon those states which can remove the embarrassments respecting the western country, a liberal surrender of a portion of their territorial claims since they cannot be preserved entire without endangering the stability of the general confederacy.

It was advised to urge upon the legislatures the indispensable necessity of establishing the federal union. The example of the New York act was commended. The states were to be urged to pass the laws for the desired cessions, and the legislature of Maryland was to be earnestly requested to authorize its delegates in Congress to subscribe the articles.

Congress took the necessary measures to carry out the provisions of this resolution. But in order to reassure the states making land cessions, that the territory entrusted to Congress would be held only for the common use and benefit of the United States in the manner contended for from the beginning of the controversy, a pledge was issued October 10, in this form:

Resolved, That the unappropriated lands that may be ceded or relinquished to the United States, by any particular state, pursuant to the recommendation of Congress of the 6th day of September last, shall be disposed of for the common benefit of the United States, and be settled and formed into distinct republican states, which shall become members of the federal union, and have the same rights of sovereignty, freedom and independence as the other states; that each state which shall be so formed shall contain a suitable extent of territory, not less than 100 nor more than 150 miles square, or as near thereto as circumstances will admit; That the necessary and reasonable expenses which any particular state shall have incurred since the commencement of the present war, in subduing any British posts, or in maintaining forts or garrisons within and for the defence, or in acquiring any part of the territory that may be ceded or relinquished to the United States, shall be reimbursed.

That the said lands shall be granted or settled at such times and under such regulations as shall hereafter be agreed on by the United States in Congress assembled, or any nine or more of them.

Two days after the adoption of this resolution in Congress, October 12, 1780, the Connecticut legislature, without knowledge of the programme

---

[33] The sequence of commitments of these papers is in a tangle on account of omissions in the journals of Congress. The original committee of October 8, John Witherspoon of New Jersey, chairman, seems to have been superseded by this committee of three, Messrs. Sherman of Connecticut, Burke of North Carolina, and Holton of Massachusetts Bay. Later a committee of seven was chosen with John Witherspoon again as chairman, and the final cessions report of November, 1781, was made by another committee of which Elias Boudinot was chairman.

therein pledged for territorial disposition, resolved to make a proportionate cession of the land claims of the state in the western country. The Connecticut resolutions proposed to surrender a portion of lands westward of the Susquehanna purchase, in compliance with the earlier recommendation, reserving full jurisdiction of the lands ceded. This was unsatisfactory as compared with the unreserved cession authorized by New York, but the resolution was not officially returned to Congress until the last day of January, by which time the third state had reported a plan of cession even more objectionable.[34]

Virginia's response to the recommendations of Congress is in the form of a resolution of the general assembly bearing date of January 2, 1781. The resolution makes no cession of territory, and confers no authority on the delegates to cede. It is merely a resolve that the commonwealth " will yield all claims " to a portion of the crown lands, on conditions which Congress was compelled to decline, for reasons expressed in the after-report of the committee, " as inconsistent with the interests of the United States, the duty Congress owes to their constituents, or the rights necessarily vested in them as the sovereign power of the United States." By the terms of the act, the assembly pledges

That this commonwealth will yield to the Congress of the United States, for the benefit of the said United States, all right, title and claim that the said commonwealth hath to the lands northwest of the river Ohio, upon the following conditions, to wit: . . .

The conditions enumerated in the resolutions aside from those expressed in the resolution of October 10, all of which are restated in the Virginia

---

[34] The method of cession proposed by Connecticut was too clumsy to admit of acceptance. The lands were to be granted direct to settlers by Connecticut for the benefit of the confederated United States, in specified estates, on survey warrants issued by Congress to grantees, as agreed to by the delegates, or any three of them. There is an attested copy of the resolution of cession in the Papers of the Continental Congress, No. 66, vol. 2, pp. 178-9. Following is a copy of the record of the action in the ms. vol. ii, Records of the State of Connecticut, October, 1780:

This Assembly taking into their Consideration a Resolution of Congress of the 6th of Septembr last recomending to the several States which have vacant unappropriated Lands lying within the Limits of their respective Charters and Claims to adopt Measures which may effectually remove the Obstacle that prevents a Ratification of the Articles of confederation together with the Papers from the States of New York Maryland & Virginia, which accompanied the same and being anxious for the accomplishment of an Event most desirable and important to the Liberty and Independence of this rising Empire, will do every Thing in their power to facilitate the same, Notwithstanding the Objection which they have to several parts of it. Resolved by this Assembly, that they will Ceed and relinquish to the United States who shall be confederated for their Use and benefit their Right or preemption of Soil in or to so much of the vacant and unapropriated Lands Claimed by this State contained and comprehended within the extent and Limits of their Charter and Grant from King Charles the second, and which lies and extends within the Limits of the same Westward of the Susquehanna Purchase so called and Eastward of the River Misisipi, as shall be in Just proportion of what shall be Ceded and relinquished by the other States, Claiming and holding vacant Lands as aforesaid with the Quantity of such their Claim unapropriated at the Time when the Congress of the United States was first convened and held at Philadelphia.

And it is further Resolved that all the Lands to be ceded and relinquished hereby, for the benefit of the Confederated United States with respect to property, but which shall nevertheless remain under the Jurisdiction of this State shall be disposed of and appropriated in such manner only as the Congress of the United states shall direct and that a Warrant under the Authority of Congress for surveying and laying out any part thereof, shall entitle the Party in whose favour it shall issue, to cause the same to be laid out and returned according to the Directions of such Warrant, and thereupon the Interest and Title of This State shall pass and be confirmed to the Grantee for the Estate specified in the said Warrant for which no other fee or reward shall be demanded or received than such as shall be allowed by Congress always provided that said Lands to be granted as aforesaid, be laid out and surveyed in Townships in regular form to a suitable number of Settlers in such manner as will best promote the Settlement and cultivation of the same according to the true spirit and principles of a Republican State. And the Delegates of this State in Congress or any three of them are hereby Impowered & Authorized in behalf of this State to agree to the Location of such Warrants and surveys as shall be made by Congress according to and in pursuance of the Resolves aforesaid and whatever may be further necessary for the same being carried into full Execution.

resolutions, include protection for the French and Canadian inhabitants of the Illinois; reservations of lands for the men of Clark's expedition and, if needed, for other soldiery of Virginia; invalidation of all Indian purchases or royal grants which are inconsistent with the chartered rights, laws, and customs of Virginia; and guaranty by the United States to the commonwealth of "all the remaining territory of Virginia included between the Atlantic ocean and the southeast side of the river Ohio, and the Maryland, Pennsylvania, and North Carolina boundaries." The "cession" was to be void and of no effect unless all the states in the American Union should ratify the articles of confederation, and it was expected in return "that every other state in the Union, under similar circumstances as to vacant territory, will make similar cessions of the same to the United States for the general emolument."

The three cessions of New York, Connecticut, and Virginia, covering practically the same lands and being so fundamentally different, required careful consideration, and Congress ordered a committee of seven to be elected to take them in charge.[35] The whole business of land concessions was relegated to this committee, where it remained until the thorough, comprehensive, and exhaustive report, which was submitted to Congress on the 3d of November, 1781, was finally disposed of in Congress eighteen months later. But while the theory and principle upon which the cessions were to stand remained officially in this prolonged state of abeyance, there was no uncertainty as to the status of the Northwest Territory. Sovereign control of the crown lands of King George was forever secure in the United States, and it remained only for the subscriptions to the definitive Treaty at Paris to make it absolute.

Maryland was now ready to enter the confederation. The cessions were made in part only, and in form wholly unsatisfactory, but with no cessions Maryland would have closed the circle of the confederacy at this juncture. The ultimate surrender of the so-called claims of individual states was inevitable; the manner and form of surrender was immaterial. It was merely a matter of courtesy, from this time on, for Congress to negotiate with particular legislatures for terms of cessions. The natural unity of interests resulting from the near approach of peace, and the certitude of a liberal allowance from the British Commissioners for peace in the boundary settlements, would have given Congress the power of assertion of control over the claimed lands if that had been necessary.[36] Other considerations impelled the state at this time—considerations of sentimental or patriotic nature—and, disregarding the cessions, the Maryland assembly ordered the name of the state to be subscribed within the thirteenth space on

---

[35] This commitment took place January 31, 1781. The journals of Congress for that day read:

A letter of the 18th, from Governor Trumbull, was read, enclosing in a resolution of the general assembly of that State, passed in October last, respecting the cession and relinquishment of the western territory to the United States,

Ordered, That the resolution of October, together with the acts and resolutions of the State of New York and the Commonwealth of Virginia, on the same subject, be referred to a committee of seven; the members, Mr. [John] Witherspoon [New Jersey], Mr. [James] Duane [New York], Mr. [Jesse] Root [Connecticut], Mr. [Samuel] Adams [Massachusetts], Mr. [John] Sullivan [New Hampshire], Mr. [Thomas] Burke [North Carolina], Mr. [George] Walton [Georgia].

The three papers named and the memorials from the earlier committee were all recommitted in July to a new committee of five, of which Elias Boudinot of New Jersey was chairman.

[36] Congress had already made assertion of supremacy in a number of cases. In addition to the interposition in the Virginia land office matter, there is the example

the scroll of the Act of Confederation. It remained only for Maryland to await with complaisance for the assured congressional control of the National domain.

The act of the Maryland assembly authorizing the ratification of the articles of confederation is in the form of a preamble and a declaration, agreed to on the 2d of February, 1781. The paper was reported to Congress and spread upon the minutes under date of February 12. The preamble tells its own story of the apprehensions which had led Maryland to the act:

> Whereas it hath been said that the common enemy is encouraged by this state not acceding to the confederation, to hope that the union of the sister states may be dissolved; and therefore prosecutes the war in expectation of an event so disgraceful to America; and our friends and illustrious ally are impressed with an idea that the common cause would be promoted by our formally acceding to the confederation; this general assembly conscious that this state hath, from the commencement of the war, strenuously exerted herself in the common cause, and fully satisfied that if no formal confederation was to take place, it is the fixed determination of this state to continue her exertions to the utmost, agreeably to the faith pledged to the Union; from an earnest desire to conciliate the affection of the sister states; to convince all the world of our unutterable resolution to support the independence of the United States, and to destroy forever any apprehensions of our friends, or hope in our enemies, of this state being again united to Great Britain.

And in order to guard the points of long contention the conditions of ratification are thus positively expressed:

> And it is hereby declared, that, by acceding to the said confederation, this state doth not relinquish, nor intend to relinquish, any right or interest she hath, with the other united or confederated states to the back country; and claim the same as fully as was done by the legislature of this state, in their declaration, which stands entered on the journals of Congress; this state relying on the justice of the several states hereafter, as to the said claim made by this state. And it is further declared, that no article in the said confederation, can or ought to bind this or any other state, to guarantee any exclusive claim of any particular state, to the soil of the said back lands, or any such claim of jurisdiction over the said lands or the inhabitants thereof.

On this firm foundation Maryland would have placed the final ratification of the confederation. Had it remained on that basis no more would have been required to place Congress in absolute control of all vacant lands and indeterminate boundaries of every state. The back line of Virginia would then have fallen at the water ridge of the Alleghanies, and the states of Kentucky and West Virginia would have had an independent organization and a more general settlement. But a conditional ratification was an impossibility without amendments that would require ratification and subscription of thirteen states. The articles must stand as ratified in Congress; they could not be affected by the conditional action of any state legislature. Maryland's signature was yet to be placed on the form of ratification, and a day was set and a programme arranged for the ceremony—March 1,

---

of the Pennsylvania-Virginia boundary disputes, wherein, on December 27, 1779, Congress resolved:

That it be recommended to the contending parties not to grant any part of the disputed land, or to disturb the possession of any persons living therein, and to avoid every appearance of force until the dispute can be amicably settled by both States, or brought to a just decision by the intervention of Congress; that possessions forcibly taken be restored to the original possessors, and things placed in the situation in which they were at the commencement of the present War, without prejudice to the claims of either party.

1781, at twelve o'clock, in Congress, when the final ratification of the confederation of the United States of America was to be announced to the public. This ceremony was carried out as arranged, and the completed articles of confederation were entered on the minutes of Congress with the signatures transcribed. But before the act of confederation could be completed by such a ceremony it was necessary to perfect the record as to the action of New York. The act of cession of the legislature of that state was accordingly spread upon the minutes. The New York delegation then executed in Congress a declaration, which was likewise entered on the journals. By this instrument the delegates declare that, being uninstructed on the subject of the Virginia guarantee by their constitutents, the cession of land and the restriction of boundary of the state of New York which they are about to make on behalf of the state, "shall not be absolute, but, on the contrary, shall be subject to ratification and disavowal by the people of the state," unless the reserved territorial rights of New York shall be guaranteed for her future jurisdiction by the United States in the same manner as stipulated by Virginia as a condition of the cession. Following this in the minutes comes the deed of restriction and absolute cession transcribed as executed in due form with legal seals and signatures all complete. The New York northern and western boundaries are given as they now exist, and the delegates:

.... cede, transfer, and forever relinquish to, and for the only use and benefit of such of the states as are or shall become parties to the articles of confederation, all the right, title, interest, jurisdiction and claim, of the state of New York, to all the lands and territories to the northward and westward of the boundaries .... to be granted and disposed of, and appropriated in such manner only, as the congress of the said United or Confederated States shall order or direct.[37]

The interest now passes to the struggle of Virginia with the committee of Congress to whom was re-committed the acts of cession and the unfinished business of the Trent and Morgan memorials. The Virginia delegation resisted a notice to appear before the committee and confer with the memorialists on the subject of their memorials, conceiving that "it derogates from the sovereignty of a state to be drawn into a contest by an individual or individuals." They inquire if Congress "intended to authorize this committee to receive claims and hear evidence in behalf of the Indiana and Vandalia Companies adverse to the claims or cessions of the states," and requested the committee to forbear the conference until Congress could advise. They appealed to Congress a second time for a ruling "on the authority of the committee to admit council or to hear documents, proofs, or evidence not among the records, nor on the files of Congress, which have not been specifically referred to them." Congress supported the committee on these rulings, and Virginia from this time on found herself deserted by her former friends in the north. Finally, in the last call of the committee for proofs, the delegates on the part of Virginia stood on their state's rights, "declining to make any elucidation of the claim, either to the lands ceded, or to the lands requested to be guaranteed to the state by Congress." The committee delayed no longer, and made final report to Congress on the 3d of November, 1781, on all matters recommitted to them.

The report of the committee of five appears in full in the journals of

---

[37] The New York deed of cession, one of twelve parchments transferred from the U. S. Department of State, is in the Division of Manuscripts, Library of Congress.

the Continental Congress for the first of May, 1782, when, after several postponements, it was on the order of the day for final discussion. It is an exhaustive report, covering all points under dispute of the right and title of the public domain, laying foundations for the land policy of the United States for all time to come. The report deals primarily with the cessions, but it does not bring the settlement of this vexatious matter. Many years must pass before all that was necessary was said and done in Congress on this subject. But while it seems to fail in securing concessions from the states in the form desired, it removed the subject from controversy, advanced the sovereignty of the United States, and fixed a *modus operandi* in territorial disposition and Indian control.

The report takes up the several cessions and claims on the basis of vouchers examined,[38] and information obtained as to the status of the lands mentioned in each; and gives the results of the findings in the form of recommendations, with reasons itemized. The findings are entirely adverse to Virginia on all points in controversy, and, according to the recommendations of the report the act of cession of the state of New York is to be accepted as based on claims of jurisdiction authentically derived from the Six United Nations of Indians. The claims of Massachusetts and Connecticut are disregarded entirely in the report, and these states are earnestly recommended "that they do without delay release all claims and pretensions of claim to the western country, without any conditions or restrictions whatever." As to Virginia, it is resolved that "Congress cannot accept of the cession proposed to be made, or guarantee the tract of country claimed by Virginia," for the reason that the lands are within the claims of other states and outside the bounds of the late colony of Virginia as it stood at the beginning of the war. It is proposed as a resolution,

That it be earnestly recommended to the state of Virginia, as they value the peace, welfare and increase of the United States, that they reconsider their said act of cession, and by a proper act for that purpose, cede to the United States all claims and pretensions of claim to the lands and country beyond a reasonable western boundary, consistent with their former acts while a colony under the power of Great Britain, and agreeable to their just rights of soil and jurisdiction at the commencement of the present war, and that free from any conditions and restrictions whatever.

Certain of the claims of the memorialists are sustained by the committee and confirmation of their purchases recommended, while others are condemned. The outline of a national Indian policy will be referred to later, as also the pledge of suitable method of opening up the territory for settlement by a new system of quadrilateral surveying based perhaps on the suggestion contained in the Connecticut resolution of cession, adopted at Hartford on the 12th of October, 1780,

Always provided that the said lands to be granted be laid out and surveyed in Townships in regular form to a suitable number of settlers, in such manner as will best promote the settlement and cultivation of the same according to the true spirit and principles of a republican state.

[38] The original ms. report of this commission is in the Papers of the Continental Congress, No. 30, pp. 15-27. There are, apparently, none of the vouchers referred to as submitted by the states in elucidation of their claims among the papers, nor can there be found " the written paper hereto annexed and numbered twenty " which the report states was delivered by the Virginia delegates on their final refusal to submit proof.

The settlement offered by the report on cessions and claims afforded the means to Congress, as the natural possessor of all the crown lands within the confines of the United States, to dispose of the same according to the pledges of the resolution of October 10, 1780. Provisions needful for such a course were contained in the report, and no determined opposition remained in Congress, save only the Virginians. In addition to the references to cessions and claims the report advises indemnification for the expenses of the Clark campaigns, recommends a policy of paternal handling of the Indians, and outlines a plan of extension of the settlements and expansion of government over the western territory. All that remained to be done, had this report endured, was for Congress, as the executive head of the United States in the exercise of right descending logically from the British crown, to proceed as convenient to carry out its provisions, to settle matters with the Indian tribes, and to dispose of all the lands from the greater mountains of the Alleghanies to Louisiana, and from Florida to Quebec, for the joint use and benefit of the United States. But Congress deliberately gave up this great advantage. The report was laid aside. No action was taken on it as a whole, and no separate part of it was ever submitted to vote. The end of the war approaching brought other mighty problems: the shifting of Congress from a martial to a civil base, and the "forming arrangements for the United States in time of peace." Examination of the minutes of Congress of this period seems to show that much of this business moved along on the theory that the land controversy was finally settled by this report.

But the Virginia delegation had never relaxed opposition to that portion of the report pertaining to their own cause. They demanded a rule requiring pledge of personal disinterest in the claims from each delegate voting, they moved for postponement whenever opportunity arose, and they constantly pressed the acceptance of the Virginia cession as a ready remedy for all the financial woes which developed in the stress of debate. For more than a year the fight kept up, and in the end the Virginians won. They secured the recommitment of that portion of the report and a final reconsideration of the question of accepting the conditional cession of the commonwealth. The New Jersey delegates filed a protest of the legislature against re-opening the question, and the Maryland delegation proposed a declaration[39] for the immediate disposition of the lands. Congress disregarded these apparently just complaints and, choosing to hold a portion only of the disputed territory, and that on a federal and not a national basis, voted on the 13th of September, 1783, to accept the Virginia cession, with all conditions approved, except the guaranty of reserved lands[40] and the invalidation of the Indian titles called for in the Virginia resolution of cession.

The action in Congress on the Virginia cession took the form of agreement to a report reviewing the eight conditions formerly named, and substantially restating them all except the guaranty and invalidation clauses,

---

[39] The New Jersey protest is entered on the minutes of Congress under date of June 20, 1783, and the Maryland declaration September 13, 1783. Later, March 1, 1784, George Morgan, the memorialist of 1779, re-appeared, demanding a hearing on his grievance "that the Commonwealth of Virginia still continued to claim the lands of the Indiana Company."

[40] The reason offered for this decision as to the guaranty is thus expressed:
Congress cannot agree to guarantee to the commonwealth of Virginia the land described in the said condition without entering into a discussion of the territorial rights of indivdual states, and only to recommend and accept a cession of their claims, whatsoever they might be, to vacant territory.

as conditions upon which the cession should be made, and recommending that "if the legislature of Virginia make a cession conformable to this report, Congress accept such cession." Quick response followed this proposal. The Virginia general assembly, October 20, 1783, "authorized their delegates to convey to the United States in Congress assembled, all the right of that commonwealth, to the territory north-westward of the river Ohio." And the delegates did so, on the 1st day of March following, by a proper deed of conveyance drawn on parchment in due form.[41] Meanwhile preparations to enter and occupy the hostile region across the Ohio were in active progress in Congress, and little attention was spared for further details of the cessions. Acts of cession followed in time from all the claimant states, but not without renewed pressure[42] on the legislatures and considerable anxiety as to the form of the cessions. But the extent and conditions of the various cessions are well known matters of history, and the dates and circumstances of each act are easy matters of reference. Weightier business was now pressing for attention in Congress. Enough had been done already respecting the title to justify immediate perfection of the programme of expansion of the government upon that part of the crown lands which had been relinquished to the United States by the cessions of New York and Virginia.

At the first signs of the coming of peace with Great Britain, Congress turned to consider the Indian preliminary to the formal occupation of his hunting grounds. The Indian policy outlined in the report on cessions and claims was ready at hand. This was merely a brief expression of the relations long subsisting in the colonies, and now recommended as a means of more clearly defining and establishing the jurisdiction of Congress regarding Indian affairs. It declares

That the sole right of superintending, protecting, treating with, and making purchases of the Indian nations outside the state lines, is necessarily vested in Congress for the benefit of the United States, that no person in separate capacity can, or ought to purchase any unappropriated lands belonging to the Indians, and that Congress has no claim in point of property of soil to lands belonging to the Indians unless the same has been *bona fide* purchased of them, or shall be purchased by Congress, and that at a public treaty to be held for that purpose.

But before such a policy could be applied to the extensive regions beyond the western frontiers matters had to be settled with the hostile nations, who, abandoned by their late allies, were left stranded on the conquered territory.[43]

"Letters from the Commander in Chief, and from the Generals" were read in Congress, while the measures for cessation of hostilities were being drawn, "informing of the sentiments of the Indians" in camp and on the

---

[41] The deed of Virginia is among the cession papers previously referred to in the Library of Congress, Division of Manuscripts; also the deeds of cession of Massachusetts, executed April 19, 1785, Connecticut, September 13, 1786, South Carolina, August 9, 1787, Connecticut, December 21, 1793, Connecticut, May 30, 1800, and Georgia, April 24, 1802. In some cases a certified copy of the legislative act of cession accompanies the deed.

[42] Resolutions of Congress agreed to April 18, 1783, and April 26, 1784.

[43] The Indians complained that they had not been consulted in the negotiations for peace and declared they were not represented in the convention at Paris which had signed away "their Island." They professed that belts had been exchanged with the Red-coats on an agreement "never to surrender their lands to the Americans," and they pointed to the proclamation of 1763 as a guarantee of their hunting grounds. Cf. Indian papers in the Papers of the Continental Congress.

British side. Agents were despatched at once to the northern and western frontiers to gather more news from the British posts. As soon as peace was announced a resolution was agreed to in Congress ordering

> That the Secretary at War take the most effectual measures to inform the several Indian nations, on the frontiers of the United States, that preliminary articles of peace have been agreed on, and hostilities have ceased with Great Britain, and to communicate to them that the forts within the United States, and in possession of the British troops, will speedily be evacuated; intimating also that the United States are disposed to enter into friendly treaty with the different tribes; and to inform the hostile Indian nations that unless they immediately cease all hostilities against the citizens of these states, and accept of these friendly proffers of peace, Congress will take the most decided measures to compel them thereto.

A committee, of which James Duane of New York was chairman, was appointed to take the Indian situation into consideration and report thereon. Meantime, to save the territory from invasion of settlers and to shield the Indian from molestation until negotiations were concluded, an ordinance was passed, September 22, and a proclamation issued prohibiting the settlement and purchase of lands inhabited or claimed by the Indians. The Duane report was ready the following month. It reviews the sentiments of the Indians and considers the situation from their standpoint, refers to their resentment against their late allies, and the natural advantage to the Americans which might be made of this feeling as a protection on the Canadian frontiers. It estimates the effect of continuing hostilities with the Indians "until all are driven into the protection of the British posts," and recommends a peaceable settlement by friendly negotiations with all nations of Indians on the basis of a waiver by Congress of the rights of conquest of the Indian lands and "atonement made by the Indians of the enormities which they have perpetrated and a reasonable compensation for the expenses which the United States have incurred by their wanton barbarities." It was proposed to ascertain and fix lines of property for the Indians, by purchase if necessary, in which care ought to be taken neither to yield nor require too much; to accommodate the Indians as far as the public will admit and to give some compensation for claims rather than to hazard a war which will be much more expensive. Conventions for this purpose were suggested to be held at various posts, and an ordinance to regulate trade, with many items particularizing how trade should be carried on. The report further declares

> That nothing can avert the complicated and impending mischiefs, or secure to the United States the just and important advantages which they ought to derive from those territories, but the speedy establishment of government and the regular administration of justice in such district thereof as shall be judged most convenient for immediate settlement and cultivation.

As may well be supposed, this enlightened report met with general acceptance in Congress. Difference of opinion developed on one point only A resolution proposing a committee to report on the expediency of laying out a suitable district within the territory, and erecting it into a distinct government, etc., for settlement, gave way, after some debate, to a substitute offered by Elbridge Gerry of Massachusetts, recommending prompt action in thus extending the government over the territory in advance of settlement without intervention of a committee to investigate its expediency.

The main body of the report was agreed to, and the committee was continued to frame an ordinance to regulate the Indian trade, and to draw up details of instruction for the treaty conventions.[44] As soon as the Virginia cession was concluded, these measures, with some alterations, were put into operation. Five Commissioners were elected March 4, 1784,

> to negotiate with the Indians in the northern and western departments, who have taken up arms against the United States, for the purpose of receiving them into the favor and protection of the United States, and of establishing boundary lines of property for separating and dividing the settlements of the citizens from the Indian villages, and hunting grounds, and thereby extinguishing as far as possible all occasion for future animosities, disquiet and contention.

It was resolved that the negotiations should commence as soon as possible, and the commissioners were "desired to meet in New York, April 10, and fix upon times and places for holding the treaties with the different nations and tribes of Indians." All prior appointments were revoked, and a form of commission was ordered to be prepared and laid before Congress by the secretary, making any three of the commissioners competent to the business of their commission. Thus began the series of purchase treaties, starting at Fort Stanwix, whereby the United States fixed forever the legal status of the American Indian, set him up on reservations, under precarious conditions of intercourse with his neighbors, citizens of the republic.[45]

Preparations for extending the settlements upon the new land were developing in Congress while the Indian matter was still under consideration. The recommendations of the Gerry resolution on this subject were expanded into a plan for a temporary government to apply to as much of the western territory as the cessions and Indian purchases would admit. This was in accordance with the pledge of October 10, 1780, and in conformity with the report on cessions and claims filed November 3, 1781, which provided for the erection "of a new state or states not exceeding 150 miles square, to be taken into the federal union, and the same to be laid out into townships of the quantity of about six miles square." All reasonable engagements for lands to the military were to be made good, and *bona fide* settlers were to be "confirmed in their title to their reasonable settlements, on the same terms as new settlements." This plan was taken up in Congress immediately after the Virginia cession, and recommitted for further consideration. A plan was reported by the committee April 19, 1784, and passed after four days debate and considerable amendment, providing for division of the territory into two distinct states by parallels of latitude and

---

[44] The Duane report, somewhat curtailed in form, is in the minutes of Congress under date of passage, October 15, 1783. The original complete drafts may be found in the Papers of the Continental Congress, No. 30. The Gerry substitute resolution reads:

Resolved, That it will be wise and necessary, as soon as circumstances shall permit, to erect a district of the western territory into a distinct government, as well for doing justice to the Army of the United States, who are entitled to lands as a bounty, or in reward of their services, as for the accommodation of such as may incline to become purchasers and inhabitants; and in the interim, that a committee be appointed to report a plan, consistent with the principles of the confederation, for connecting with the Union by a temporary government, the purchasers and inhabitants of the said district, until their number and circumstances shall entitle them to form a permanent constitution for themselves, and as citizens of a free, sovereign and independent state, to be admitted to a representation in the Union; provided always, that such constitution shall not be incompatible with the republican principles, which are the basis of the constitution of the respective states of the Union.

[45] The commissioners first to serve were George Rogers Clark, Oliver Wolcott, and Richard Butler; Arthur Lee, elected April 24, 1784; and Samuel Holden Parsons, elected September 21, 1785. The original commission issued to General Parsons is in the manuscript collections of the Western Reserve Historical Society.

meridians of longitude. A number of forms of this ordinance, found among the papers of Congress, are of curious interest. No attempt was made to put the plan into practice. In fact, all these first efforts at providing a government for a fanciful state in the midst of an unbroken forest were abandoned as premature. The Indian treaties were not yet settled, and the actual purchase of soil had not been made. So all plans were dropped for another year, and when they appeared again the subject matter of the plan was divided, and there were two separate ordinances—one the land ordinance of 1785, and the other the famous Ordinance of 1787.

The land ordinance of May 20, 1785, made its preliminary appearance in Congress early in March and passed through several commitments until reported April 14 by a grand committee in a form "for ascertaining the mode of disposing of lands in the western territory." Thereafter the ordinance was the subject of continuous attention until its final passage in amended condition.[46] This is the act which the states had long desired, to open the coveted lands of the Ohio. It defines a mode of subdividing the territory into small parcels for quick sale, and names for the first offer a most desirable section. The price is low per acre, to insure a ready market, and the terms easy, to fit the infirmities of the times. The act thus made favorable was passed to meet a public exigency, and its application was hastened to satisfy a suppositive demand, which never existed, and to supply a quick revenue, which never came. The subdivision of the soil into small areas was made in the wilderness in heroic manner, as ordered, and the lands were offered at public vendue to save time and trouble for purchasers, but the sales were so few, and the returns in funds so inconsiderable, that the event itself is nearly forgotten and its traces in the records are almost entirely lost.

The land ordinance of 1785 inaugurated a system of surveying which was afterward perfected by practice and experience into that now in use in almost every civilized country on earth. It replaced the customary method of the ages, of locating by metes and bounds. The returns of homestead settlement by description referring to familiar objects of the landscape— so much frontage on a river or lake, including so many acres, by lines running to a tree or mountain as near as may be—would not apply in an unknown wilderness. An exact rule was needed of locating accurately, determinable by rod and chain, projected from an astronomical point whereby "the homesteader could locate his hut by the stars of heaven, no longer dependent on the whim or caprice of the overlord." The parcels were to be "squares" formed by parallels and meridians, the lines run by the compass and marked by chops on the trees as numbered towns and ranges, the whole presentable in a checkered plat, from which the purchaser might select his site. The first suggestion of the original ordinance made these squares "hundreds," ten miles on a side, with one hundred interior squares or lots of 640 acres each. The draft of April 26 reduces the township to seven miles, with forty-nine interior lots, and the final ordinance makes a further reduction to thirty-six lots, as now in use.[47]

[46] The ordinance is entered on the minutes of Congress under date of April 26, and again with the alterations on the date of its passage, May 20, 1785.

[47] This remarkable device of surveying, now known as the rectangular system, and called "one of America's greatest inventions" (W. R. H. S. Tract No. 61, p. 282), has not been traced to its origin. If the thread is ever picked up it will doubtless be found running through the New England village of geometrically exact form. It has been said that Jefferson devised the scheme, but this would not explain the Connecticut suggestion of October 12, 1780, nor the recommendation in the report of November 3,

Immediate attention to the enforcement of the land ordinance follows its enactment. On the seventh day after passage, May 27, 1785, "The Geographer of the United States (Captain Thomas Hutchins) was continued in his office for a term of three years, at an allowance of six dollars a day for his services and expenses," and, according to order, Congress proceeded on the same day to the election of a surveyor for each state.[48] This action was taken in the reasonable expectation that the Indian programme settled upon would be carried out by the commissioners elected, the object being to obtain from the northern and western nations and tribes consent in writing to the extinguishment of their rights to the federal lands intended for settlement, and substantial engagements for the establishment of permanent relations of peace and friendship between the Indian and the settler.[49] The treaty at Fort Stanwix, October 27, 1784, settled matters on this basis with the northern Indians, and by a similar treaty at Fort McIntosh, January 21, 1785, the commissioners gained the consent of the western tribes[50] to the survey and settlement of the lands as far westward as the division line drawn between the portages of the Cuyahoga and the Great Miami rivers. These two great conventions, conducted with much show of dignity and considerable display of military protection, with great consumption of stores and exchanges of cash for wampum,

---

1781. Most likely it arose naturally from many sources to meet a general want. A curious pamphlet of the 18th century seems to bear out this idea:

"Britania Major, the New Scheme, or Essay, for discharging the debts, improving the lands, and enlarging the trade, of the British Dominions in Europe and America," London, 1732.

The unknown author of this most remarkable book, in elaborating a plan for the exchange of the "useless and unimproved lands of the British Isles and Northern America" with the creditors of the Nation, in the form of manors of 3000 plantation acres each to the nobility suitably graded, proposes, "a new division of each Province to be made into *Counties* of about 33 *Square Miles*, the *County Town* to be near the Centre, and each *County* to be divided into a proper number of *Hundreds* and *Parishes*. All the lands aforesaid to be measured out in *Squares*, and divided into Parishes as convenience of Habitation shall require." (p. 31.)

[48] Under the ordinance Congress elected surveyors on the 27th of May and subsequently, and their names were proposed by delegates from the several states as follows: *Massachusetts*: Rufus Putnam, excused, no service; Benjamin Tupper, elected July 18, "with authority to perform the duties of that office until Mr. Putnam shall actually join the Geographer and take the same upon himself," served 1785, 1786, 1787. *New York*: William [W.] Morris, served 1785, 1786. *Virginia*: Alexander Parker, served 1785, 1786. *Maryland*: James Simpson, served 1785, 1786, 1787. *New Hampshire*: Nathaniel Adams, declined; Ebenezer Sullivan, August 15, declined; Edward Dowse, August 24, served 1785, resigned; Winthrop Sargent, June 27, 1786, served, 1786. *Rhode Island*: Caleb Harris, declined; Ebenezer Sproat, May 22, 1786, served 1786, 1787. *Pennsylvania*: Adam Hoops served 1785. *North Carolina*: Absalom Tatum, no service. *South Carolina*: William Tate, no service. *Georgia*: Robert Johnson, June 20, served 1785, 1786. *New Jersey*: Absalom Martin, June 20, served 1785, 1786, 1787. *Connecticut*: Isaac Sherman, June 27, served 1785, 1786, 1787. *Delaware*: Mark McCall, July 15, no service.

[49] Albert Gallatin thus states the situation of the treaty nations:
Those tribes are in some respects considered as independent communities. They govern themselves without being subject to the laws of the United States; and their right to remain in possession of the lands they occupy, and to sell them only when they please is recognized. On the other hand the United States have the exclusive right of pre-emption, and all sales to foreign nations or to individuals, whether citizens or foreigners, are null by law; a provision as necessary for the protection of the Indians, as for that of the public domain. The principle is generally acknowledged by themselves and recognized in several of their treaties. Nor can it be disputed that even if their own right to sell is entire, the United States have that to forbid any one to purchase. The sales to the United States are however altogether voluntary and never made without a compensation more valuable to the Indians than the use of the land which they cede. (Introduction to Laws, Treaties and other Documents having operation and respect to the public Lands, collected and arranged pursuant to an act of Congress, passed April 27, 1810, Washington City. Printed by Joseph Gales, Jun., p. xiv.)

[50] The Wyandot, Delaware, Chippewa, and Ottawa tribes. The full text of these two treaties is recorded in the minutes of Congress for June 3, 1785.

were deemed sufficient to insure pacific conditions for the land surveys. But, "in order to give greater security to the frontier settlements, and establish a boundary line between the United States and the Potawatoma, Twightwees, Plankishaw and other western nations," Congress ordered a treaty, March 17, to be held with these Indians " at post Vincent on the Wabash river, on the 20th day of June or at such time or place as the commissioners may find most convenient." Even with these treaties there would still remain some uncertainty as to how the Shawnees would regard the transfer of their lands made at Fort Stanwix and Fort McIntosh, and a special treaty with these tribes was ordered by Congress, June 29, " to be held on the western bank of the Ohio, at the rapids, or at the mouth of the Great Miami," and arrangements were made for the commissioners and military to attend.[51]

Trusting that these accommodations would clear the frontiers of danger for the execution of the land ordinance, Captain Hutchins rendezvoused his men at Pittsburgh, the nearest point of approach to the scene of the surveys, where he arrived September 3, 1785. Accounts current there respecting the Indians were so very vague, uncertain, and unfavorable, that he took counsel with the commandant at Fort McIntosh, who was of the opinion " that he might very safely repair with the surveyors to the intersection of the west line of Pennsylvania with the Ohio," where he was to begin the survey. Here, also, he met and counselled with General Butler en route to the Shawnee meeting, and despatched a courier to the Indian towns "requesting a chief from each of the Delaware and Wyandott nations for the purpose of constantly attending the surveyors during their being employed in the western territory;" and having written to the President of Congress of his intentions, Capt. Hutchins took the current of the Ohio, on September 22, for the place fixed by the land ordinance as the starting point of the survey.[52]

Arriving at Little Beaver Creek the geographer-general made camp at the " point on the River Ohio found to be due north from the western termination of a line, which has been run as the southern boundary of the state of Pennsylvania," there to await the return of his messengers and the arrival of the chiefs for his escort. During the intermediate time he took account of his equipment for the survey, " ascertained the variation of the different compasses belonging to the surveyors, and also the difference in the lengths of their Gunther's chains."[53] He endeavored also " to find out the true variation of the needle and the latitude of the point of beginning the east and west line, and from a mean of a great number of observations

[51] Gen. Samuel H. Parsons joined General Clark and General Butler as commissioners for this treaty.

[52] As the letter despatched from Pittsburg to Congress was the first he had written since receiving the copies of the ordinance which he was to put into operation, the Geographer took the occasion to observe:

By the Ordinance of Congress I am Commanded to lay off each Township Six Miles Square, by Lines running due North & South, and others crossing these at right angles as near as may be; Permit me to observe that as we approach the Pole the Meridians have a gradual inclination towards each other until they terminate in a point, therefore Six Miles square cannot be comprehended within the Meridians, and it will be impossible for each Township to contain 23,040 Acres as intended by Congress without adding in Latitude what may be wanting in Longitude.—I pray to be honored with Instructions on this Matter as soon as Congress shall think proper should they deem it necessary to give directions at all, in the meantime I will proceed as directed in the Ordinance.

[53] No special instruments were provided by the United States for the public surveys until they were called for in 1804 by Surveyor-General Jared Mansfield to correct the error made by the Connecticut surveyors in running the south line of the Western Reserve.

both on the sun and north star made the latitude 40°: 38′: 02″ north, and the variation of the compass 54′ east." Disquieting rumors of the Indians came to him from the neighborhood, but so great was his anxiety to carry the ordinance into execution that, on the 30th of September, he commenced running the first east and west line, notwithstanding disagreeable reports heard of "many prisoners and scalps taken into the Shawanoese towns by Indians unknown, and of a man and a part of his family killed and scalped a few miles below his encampment."

Captain Hutchins advanced less than four miles on the east and west line, purposely holding back in fear of the hovering Indians, and in anxiety for the return of the messenger with the protecting escort of chiefs. He remained on the line until October 9, when news of the threatening Indians brought in by one of the surveyors caused him to suspend operations and remove the camp to the southern side of the river.[54] There on the 15th of October he received the returning messenger laden with most unfriendly intelligence from the Indian towns. So far from meeting him at the appointed place, there were orders from the tribes who, at the Fort McIntosh convention, had "consented to the cessions and promised cooperation," for "Captain Hutchins and Brothers who sit at the thirteen fires . . . to desist from prosecuting the surveying business until the treaty to be held at the big Miami river."[55]

Thus ended the first attempt of the United States to survey the federal lands. The geographer removed his outfit to Pittsburgh, and later departed for New York. In a letter dated November 25 he communicated these facts to the President of Congress, enclosing all papers respecting Indian matters gathered while on the frontiers.

A few weeks after his return to New York, Captain Hutchins transmitted to Congress

a plan and Remarks of that part of the Western Territory through which an East and West Line has been run, agreeable to an ordinance of Congress of the 20th of May last. The plan was copied from the original by Mr. William Morris Surveyor appointed by Congress from the State of New York. The justice I owe that Gentlemans merit and abilities, as well as for the active part which he took in forwarding of and assisting in the astronomical business of the Geographic Department when in the Western Territory, will I hope be admitted as a sufficient apology, for my having taken the liberty of mentioning his Name on the occasion.[56]

The letters of Captain Hutchins, and the papers accompanying them, give an explanation of the violation of the treaty by the Ohio Indians. In the letter sent to Congress from Pittsburgh, September 15, he declares:

This place is destitute of any accounts from De Troit or Niagara.—Permit me to assure your excellency, that, whilst the British possess those Posts, all Negociations with the Indian Nations on the part of the United States will fall far short of the end proposed to be attained, neither will Congress have that

---

[54] While waiting at the new encampment opposite the Little Beaver River camp, the geographer "made as many observations on the sun and north star as sufficiently enabled him to determine the latitude to be 40°: 37′: 47″ and the variation of the compass about the same as on the North side of the river."

[55] Letter spoken by Captain Pipe for the Delawares and Wyandotts, at Upper Sandusky, October 5, 1785. Papers of the Continental Congress, No. 60, p. 209.

[56] Letter dated New York 27th Decemr., 1785. Papers of the Continental Congress, No. 60, p. 225. The Remarks follow the letter (pp. 229–39), but the plan is missing. No plan of Hutchins's work in the Seven Ranges of Townships has been located, but there are many letters and papers pertaining to the surveys in this volume.

weight & Influence in the Councils of the Indian Nations, not even in those situated nearest to Pittsburgh, which the very great expence and trouble, that August Body have taken ought to insure to them;—Indeed these circumstances together with the evil reports industriously propagated amongst the Indians by a number of persons who have in defiance of the Proclamation of Congress settled on the north side of the Ohio near to the Mingo Town 75 Miles below Pittsburgh, will greatly contribute to alienate the affections of the Indians, who, if freed from evil councellors, would be desirous of living peaceably and friendly with the Citizens of the United States. This is an Evil, allow me to say, which calls loudly for immediate redress, more especially as, in my opinion, the Surveyors have reason to apprehend much greater danger from those disorderly Persons, than from the Indians themselves.[57]

Information gathered at Little Beaver creek seems to support this theory. One witness reported:

Wyandots told the Delawares it was an open war; the British had sent tomahawks among them and that all the nations meant to strike. On the 1st of October they arrived, at which time, a grand council of the chiefs of the following nations was held at the Delaware town on the headwaters of the great Miami, vizt. the Wyandots, Delawares, Mingoes, Shawneese, Cherokees, Potutawatamies Miamies and Twightwees. The Kickapoos, Wauweaughtenies, Fox, Ottaway, Chepawa nations were not present but they sent their speeches with their wampum. That he was informed their intention at this meeting was to brighten the chain of friendship, and bind their union the firmer; ... that he saw a man who wishes his name to be kept secret, who told him the British were using their influence to prevent the Indians from attending the treaty at the mouth of the Great Miami.

It was reported also that the Wyandots and Delawares, after their return from Fort McIntosh, had received communications from Detroit in which the British denied having given their country away; they acknowledged they had made peace with the Americans and agreed to a boundary line between them, and had also given the Americans the laws or jurisdiction over the country, but they did not give them any right to the land.[58]

The initial point of the survey, fixed by the land ordinance, as

a point that shall be found to be due north from the western termination of a line, which has been run as the southern boundary of the state of Pennsylvania,

was easily located by the geographer, through observation of the markings made south of the Ohio river by commissioners of Pennsylvania then employed in running the west boundary line of the commonwealth. Captain Hutchins was himself engaged for this work, having been employed during the previous summer in determining the western extent of the southern boundary line of Pennsylvania, and he would have continued, but for his present labors, in running a north line from that point as far as the Ohio River. From this point he ran the East and West Line or, as it was later

---

[57] Papers of the Continental Congress, No. 60. p. 189.
[58] The geographer favored the President of Congress with an opinion of the cause of the unexpected Indian disaffection in the territory, but it must be considered that Captain Hutchins had brought to America a great grievance against the British, and this may have affected his judgment:

When your Excellency compares all the above information and circumstances together with the repeated threats and solemn declarations of some hundreds of persons who have taken umbrage at that part of Ordinance relative to the mode of disposing of Lands in the Western Territory, and who in consequence thereof, have removed with their Families and Effects in the course of the last spring and summer to Detroit that they would irritate the Indians against the Surveyors appointed by Congress and actually go with the Indians to the War against them; permit me to hope that my conduct will appear to merit your Excellency's approbation more especially as I have made it my constant study to pursue every measure that to me appeared best calculated to enable me faithfully to discharge the trust reposed in me.—All the Indian information I could procure I have transmitted copies of to General Butler for the purpose of making his Negotiations with the Indians more successful.

called, the Geographer's Line, westward for a distance of 3 miles, 66 chains and 78 links to the place where he heard the evil news.[59]

The next year the geographer and his staff returned to the survey, intending to make up for lost time of the previous failure by completing thirteen ranges of townships ready for sale before the season closed. The return was ordered in Congress by a resolution of the 9th of May, 1786, with some opposition, and a proposition for alteration of the land ordinance. No alterations were made, however, except a provision that "the surveyors do not proceed further northerly than the east and west line,"[60] and a repeal of the clause requiring them " to pay the utmost attention to the variation of the magnetic needle and to run and note all lines by the true meridian." The treaty at the Big Miami, held on the 21st of January, had rendered everything secure—as Congress supposed.[61] The geographer set out for the frontier May 23 and, arriving at Pittsburg June 25, despatched messengers for the chiefs of the Delawares, Wyandots, and Shawnees who, " agreeable to their promise to the Commissioners, were to give him protection." He informed Congress, in a letter dated July 8, that " troops may be necessary," and he proceeded at once, without waiting for either soldiers or Indians, to resume the surveys. But when he summoned the men, who had assembled at the former camp awaiting orders, they positively refused to proceed until a body of troops was provided to cover their operations.[62]

Thus the surveys were resumed. The east and west line was projected westerly to the ninth range, a distance of over fifty miles. From this line as a base, range lines six miles apart were run southerly to the river, a distance on the westerly ranges of ninety-five miles. Cross lines were run every six miles, working westerly from the river at right angles

---

[59] No description has been found of his method of finding this point, but it may be supposed that he sighted across the river from the south shore. According to present geography the East and West Line forms the north line of the second tier of lots, or sections, of the township of Liverpool, Columbiana County, Ohio, passing directly north of the city of East Liverpool. It is not known how Capt. Hutchins marked the initial point, nor how it was situated with respect to the high- and low-water lines of the Ohio River. The original surveyor's plat of the northeasterly township of the Seven Ranges of Townships, in the General Land Office, Drafting Division, Washington, D. C., shows the point at the exact margin of the river as does also the published plat of the Seven Ranges of Townships made to advertise the sale of 1796. But maps of Ohio from that day to this show a bit of land between the line and the river, which may or may not be due to the recession of the river. Virginia has always claimed that her reserved territory extended to the high-water mark on the northerly side of Ohio River, but Chief Justice Marshall ruled (v. Wharton, 691) that low-water mark on the northwest side was the boundary of Ohio.

The Pennsylvania commissioners completed the west boundary line of Pennsylvania to Lake Erie in October, 1786, " by opening a Vista and planting stones marked P on the east side." Penn. Arch , vol. 10, pp. 440, 443, 452, 760; vol. 11, p. 69.

[60] This alteration in the field of survey, which originally extended " from the River Ohio to the lake Erie," was made in Congress after the report of the geographer of the latitude of the east and west line, 40°: 38': 02'', to accommodate the claims of Connecticut, which lay between 41° and 42°, 02;'' north latitude.

[61] The Shawnee tribes had given their signatures to the prescribed division line, and the Wyandots had sent their hostage to Congress as a token of their repentance for the broken treaty. Half King, chief of the Wyandot tribes, sent his son Scotosh to visit Congress in July. The young chief was received with ceremony. There was a conference, a speech to Congress, and a letter in which Scotosh declared 'that his father and the Wyandot nation were satisfied to have the land measured.' Papers of the Continental Congress, No. 30, pp. 381-387.

[62] Correspondence dated "Little Beaver Rivulet, July 21 and 22, 1786 Gen. Benj'n. Tupper, Surveyor of Massachnsetts, wrote the response in behalf of the surveyors present." Hutchins Papers, vol. 3, pp. 25, 26, Hist. Soc. of Penn.

to the range lines, and every mile was marked by chops on trees standing on or near the line, as required by the ordinance. The geographer and his eight surveyors and many more chainbearers, axe men, and followers, and a battalion of military to escort them, were thus spread out over the triangular field of the survey, pushing the work steadily, "even Sundays not excepted," to finish the thirteen ranges—if possible, altogether making quite a stir in the wilderness east of the Muskingum and the Tuscarawas. The storm broke upon them in September. At his camp, "38 miles on the the East and West line," Hutchins received a message from the chief of the Wyandots, informing him that they could not comply with the request to assist in the surveying until they had brought the "back nations"[63] to terms. "I am just now between two fires," spoke Half King, "for I am afraid of you and likewise of the back nations." From other sources it was learned that a large body of Indians was collecting with hostile intentions, determined "that the Ohio river and the line being cut by Pennsylvania shall remain forever the boundary between them and the Big Knives." The Shawnees had five hundred warriors ready to move the "moment they hear Captain Hutchins is out." On October 1 the danger had become so threatening that the surveyors held to camp, absolutely refusing to continue.[64] The men were in terror, and the geographer, "to his great mortification," was obliged to advise retirement to the back ranges. With great difficulty he kept enough men at work until four ranges were completed. Still the attacks continued, and in November, on advice of the military, the surveyors withdrew to a camp on the Virginia side.[65] Captain Hutchins informed Congress of the interruption of the survey in a letter dated at the Virginia camp, December 2, adding: "I shall be detained here until such time as the townships already surveyed are delineated on paper, which will probably take to the commencement of the ensuing year, when I shall lose no time in proceeding with them to New York."[66] Captain Hutchins returned to New York in February, carrying with him

[63] Meaning Ottawas, Chippewas, Potawatomies, and Miamis. Papers of the Continental Congress, No. 60, p. 254.

[64] The refusal is embodied in a round robin, signed Benj. Tupper, Wm. W. Morris, Absalom Martin, James Simpson, Samuel Montgomery, Michael Duffy, Andrew Henderson, Charles Smith. Congress has given authority to the geographer to appoint surveyors as vacancies occurred, which accounts for the last four names. The surveyors employed the first season were: Benjamin Tupper, William W. Morris, Alexander Parker, James Simpson, Robert Johnson, Isaac Sherman, Absalom Martin, and Edward Dowse. (Cf. Papers of the Continental Congress, No. 41, vol. vi, p. 301, and Minutes of Congress, date of September 25, 1786.)

[65] A letter dated October 27, 1786, informed Hutchins that "Joseph Brant with 56 of the Six Nations had gone to the Shawnees Towns. In a council he had with some of the Indians at Casheckton he expressed a wonder that the surveyors should proceed to survey the land that did not belong to them." Hutchins Papers, vol. 3, p. 32, Hist. Soc. of Penn.

[66] The ordinance required the surveyors "to mark the lines they had run on plats and to note thereon all mines, salt-springs, salt-licks, mill-sites, water-courses, mountains, and other remarkable and permanent things over and near which the lines shall pass, and also the quality of the lands," and to return these plats to the Secretary at War, who was to cause a copy thereof to be made for the loan commissioner of each state for purposes of the sale. One set only of these plats was made, consisting of 77 townships, and they are still preserved in the United States General Land Office in charge of E. Mulkow, a veteran employee who rescued them some years ago from destruction by mildew when the General Land Office was removed from the Patent Office building to its present quarters. Each of these plats is signed by the surveyor. They are drawn on a scale of 40 chains to the inch, and the interior lines forming 36 lots, which were not run by the surveyors are ruled on certain of the plats, to show the results of sales. There is also a book of exteriors of certain townships, with elaborate descriptions, which seem to belong to this survey.

the visible and tangible evidence of his labors. "I have brought with me," he wrote to the President of Congress, "the plats and description of four ranges completely surveyed containing in the whole six hundred and seventy-five thousand four hundred and eighty acres." These he deposited with the board of treasury, according to the ordinance; and on the 18th of April he sent his own returns to Congress.

Captain Hutchins's returns were the subject of immediate action in Congress, in the consideration of "a plan for selling for public securities the townships surveyed in the western territory" reported by the board of treasury on the 19th of April. The report condemns the plan of proportional distribution by states through the Secretary at War and the local loan offices, fixed in the ordinance to take place "as soon as 7 ranges of townships shall have been surveyed," as too slow and expensive, and recommends a direct sale at public auction to the highest bidder regardless of his local habitation. Congress agreed to this report April 21, and ordered "the sale to be advertised to commence at the expiration of five months from date, in the place where Congress shall sit and continue from day to day until the same shall be sold." The advertisements appeared as directed.[67] Twenty-seven separate townships or fractional townships are listed in a table by range and township numbers, to be exposed to sale, either entire or in lots (now called sections) of one mile square in alternate order, at not less than one dollar per acre, plus cost of surveying, payable one third down and the remaining two thirds in three months, in specie, or certificates, "excepting therefrom and reserving one third part of all gold, silver, lead and copper mines within the land sold."[68] Proper maps and descriptions of the lands were to be exhibited at the time and place of sale, and the sales were to continue from day to day until the whole were sold. "The admirable quality of these lands, and the favorable climate in which they are situated," the advertisements declare, "are too well known to need description."

The sale took place as advertised, in New York, September 21, 1787, continuing until October 9, when it ceased, with the greater part of the townships remaining unsold. During the sixteen days of sale 32 persons bought 148 parcels, aggregating 150,896 acres, 176,090 6/90th dollars, purchase money, of which 87,438 18/90th dollars was paid at the time of sale in public securities.[69] The highest price bid was 22 dollars for a fractional lot of an acre and a half on the river, but most of the sales were at the minimum rate of a dollar per acre. During the summer of 1787, the surveyors again returned to the Ohio. Troubles with the Indians had not abated, but they finished closing in the townships of seven ranges. Hutchins probably did not attend this survey as he was in New York in October busy with his accounts. He made final report the following summer and turned in the finished plan of the Seven Ranges, which he transmitted to the board of treasury under date of July 26, 1788.

[67] The order was to advertise the sale "in one of the newspapers at least of each of the states." See *N. Y. Packet*, May 15, 1787; *Providence Gazette*, Aug. 11, 18, 25, Sept. 1; *Connecticut Courant*, June 25, July 9, 23, Aug. 6; *Pennsylvania Packet*, Sept. 6, 13, 18, etc.

[68] This reservation still stands as a lien on the lands. It is entered on the patents issued at the time by the board of treasury, and is recorded in the county books of Ohio where the lands are situated. This clause was omitted from the act of 1796.

[69] Albert Gallatin gives the results of the New York sale, in a summary printed in the Introduction to the Land Laws, p. xxii, previously referred to, as "72,974 acres at public sale at New York, in the year 1787, for 87,325 dollars, in evidence of the public debt," while Public Domain, p. 17, gives other figures.

The circumstances of the first survey and sale of the federal lands, from which so much had long been expected and so little realized, would be interesting and doubtless important if all were known, but scarcely anything remains of this period in the public prints or official records to tell the story. The sale itself was a failure and the survey a disappointment. The first returns of four ranges, after years of waiting, expense, and danger, were so meagre as to justify criticism in Congress of the mode of survey, and call for immediate revision of the ordinance, and a move in that direction is noted in the minutes of Congress at the time the sale was ordered.[70] At this very moment, also, memorials began to appear, praying Congress for grants of large areas for private adventure in settlement for which large sums of money were promised for immediate payments, offering quicker means of revenue than the auction sales.[71] Hutchins's finished plan and description of the whole Seven Ranges came in during the summer of 1788,[72] but there the business dropped. By that time several

[70] It was recommended in April, 1787, "that Congress adopt measures for disposing of the lands which may be, not only practicable, but speedy in their operation." An investigation of the working of the geographer's department under the ordinance followed, and a revision appeared of the old ordinance, providing, for private adventures in locating, surveying, and settling lands, conformable, in a fashion, to the six mile township system. The revision gained no standing in Congress, as it was deemed best not to interfere with sales depending, both public and private, by new legislation of this nature. But after the sales were over the subject was revived, and a supplemental ordinance was passed July 9, 1788, repealing parts deemed objectionable in the old ordinance, suspending the public sales at the option of the board of treasury, and authorizing the private locations provided for in the former revision, with respect to the two military tracts westward of the Seven Ranges of Townships, which, on the 22d of October, 1787, were designated by act of Congress for apportionment as army lands. (The revised draft of April, 1787, is in the Papers of the Continental Congress, No. 30, p. 119.)

[71] The first of these proposals is the Memorial of the Associators, in the handwriting and over the signature of their Agent, "Sam H. Parsons." Dated in New York the 8th of May, 1787, read in Congress May 9, reported by the committee July 10, it was discussed and acted on July 23, when it was referred to the board of treasury to take order. This was the earliest explicit offer of money for lands, but the contract was not closed. Dr. Manasseh Cutler, one of the Association, filed another memorial on July 6, which was acted on in the same way July 27, and this was made the basis of the contract with the Ohio Company of Associates. Next came the proposition of William Duer, agent for the Scioto Company, which, for prudential reasons, was combined with the contract of the Ohio Company. (The Parsons memorial is in the Papers of the Continental Congress, No. 41, vol. viii, p. 226; and the committee report, No. 19, vol. v, p. 27. The letter of Dr. Cutler, dated Ipswich, Nov. 19, 1788, explaining the Scioto land transaction, is among the Col. John May papers, W. R. H. S. Cf. also the Memorial of the Directors of the Ohio Company, dated March 2, 1792, W. R. H. S.)
There is a prior proposition dated July 16, 1783, a "petition of the Subscribers Officers in the Continental Line of the Army," praying for the locating of their military lands on Lake Erie, "on conditions of settlement and purchase, for public securities," but this was too early to receive recognition. (The petition with nearly 300 signatures is in the Papers of the Continental Congress, No. 42, vol. vi, p. 65.)
A curious petition was filed in Congress in October, 1784, "of the inhabitants residing near the Ohio River, praying that each one may be indulged with taking out warrants according to his abilities and locating the same in what manner they shall see fit." Ibid., No. 42, vol. vi, p. 106.

[72] This letter was found by the writer in the attic of the General Land Office. It is now in the file room, Surveyor's Division, General Land Office.

                                                              New York, 26th July, 1788.
Gentlemen:
You will receive herewith a Plan of the Seven Ranges containing 1.641.724 acres with the surveys and Descriptions appertaining thereto, also a calculation of the Townships and Fractional parts of Townships in the Fifth, Sixth and Seventh Ranges.
    I am very Respectfully
        Gentlemen
            Your most obedient servant
                THO: HUTCHINS.
    The Honble Commissioners of the board of Treasury.

The plan is missing, but the descriptions and calculation were found with the letter.

large purchases had been successfully concluded by the board of treasury, beginning with the Ohio Company of Associates, which was closed a few weeks after the end of the New York sales. All dealings for lands ceased under the new constitution until, after the Greenville Treaty, the act of Congress of 1796 restored the system inaugurated by Captain Hutchins into full force and effect.[73]

Official returns of the New York sale are found in the papers of the Continental Congress, entitled:

Schedule of Sales of Lands in the Western Territory of the United States, at Public Auction, from the 21st Septemr. to the 9t. October 1787—And the Amount of Public Securities received in payment for the Same.

This document, consisting of six large tabulated sheets, signed by M. Hillegas, U. S. Treasurer, and Wm. Duer, Secretary of the board of treasury, and dated September 13, 1788, gives names of each purchaser, township and lot number, acreage, amount paid etc.[74] There is also in the land office in Washington the book of patents issued for the sale, in which the names and dates of the complete purchases are given.[75] In addition are the surveyors plats, previously mentioned, on which are recorded the names and other data of sales. Finally there are the lands themselves entered in the several counties in Ohio, with records of the original purchasers. From all these sources it is possible to compile a list of the first owners of public lands of the United States.

It is possible also to give a correct list of the 1000 original proprietors and settlers of the Muskingum settlement of the Ohio Company from the official records of draughts and allotments of lands to each proprietor, kept by Col. John May, secretary of the Ohio Company, and recently found. The draughts took place at Providence, R. I., on Thursday, the 8th of May, 1787, and on the Muskingum in July, 1788. (Cf. Cutler's Journal, also the Journal of Col. John May.)[76]

The lists of names of first owners of lands within the limits of the State of Ohio, as proposed on an earlier page of this writing, here follow. They

---

[73] The board of treasury had authority to hold a public sale at any time or place of the land remaining unsold in the Seven Ranges of Townships after the New York sale, but no more lots were sold until 1796, when the Secretary of the Treasury held sales under the first land law of Congress (May 18, 1796), as follows: at Pittsburgh, where alternate townships were offered for sale in lots, or sections, and 43,446 acres were sold for 100,427 dollars; and at Philadelphia, where the alternate townships entire were offered, and one sale made, 5,200 acres at $2.00 per acre. No other sales were made of public lands until the establishment of the local land office system by the act of May 10, 1800. The latest larger histories are at fault on this matter of the early land sales. (Cf. act of May 18, 1796, and Introduction to the Land Laws, p. xxii.)

[N. B. The writer wishes to acknowledge his obligations to Mr. T. L. Cole, of Washington, D. C., for generous use of his large and valuable collection of state and colonial laws.]

[74] No. 59, vol. 3, p. 135.

[75] In the Recorder's Division. The binder's title of this volume is as follows: Miscellaneous Vol. 1, Record of Patents, Sales at New York, Vol. A, Credit, General Land Office.

[76] A number of alphabetical lists of proprietors, and separate lists of drafts, found among the papers of Col. John May are in the New England Historic Genealogical Society, Boston, and the Western Reserve Historical Society, Cleveland.

are constructed for the purpose of this publication by comparison of the several documents mentioned.[77]

First Owners of Lands in Ohio

The sale of lots or the Four Ranges of Townships at public vendue in the City of New York, September 21 to October 9, 1787, terminated the period of reservation or prohibition of "settlement and purchase of the lands inhabited or claimed by the Indians."[78] Purchasers of lots at this sale obtained thereby the right of entry and occupancy of the lands that they had purchased; all others were trespassers, excepting the French and Canadians in the Illinois Company, who were protected by their oath of fidelity to Virginia.[79] These purchasers received certificates of payment of purchase money issued by the Treasurer of the United States,[80] which entitled them to such right. Certain purchasers, no doubt, moved at once upon their lands, probably from the vantage camps on the Virginia hills overlooking the forbidden river, but other purchasers made no actual settlements; facts to be ascertained by those especially interested.[81] Their names appear in the Schedule of Sales returned by the Treasurer of the United States after full payment for the lots had been made, as ordained by the act of Congress passed May 20, 1785. They appear also, except the forfeitures for non-payment of purchase money, in the official Record of Patents, and on the plats of the surveyors, to which reference has been made.

The Schedule of Sales contains the names of purchasers with other data, in order as the sales were made; description of each lot sold; location by numerals to indicate the range, township, and lot; number of acres in each lot; amount of purchase price; payments made, etc. The Record of Sales is a volume made up of printed blanks used by the Board of Treasury for recording the patents as issued, one full page for each lot patented. The pages are numbered progressively and dated as filled out, and the blanks are filled in with name and other data corresponding with the items of the Schedule of Sales.[82] The plats of the surveyors show the exteriors

---

[77] Cf. Register for October, 1910, p. 369.

[78] As proclaimed according to Act of Congress passed September 22, 1783, entitled "An ordinance prohibiting settlement and purchase of certain lands."

[79] Cf. Register for April, 1910, p. 268.

[80] Cf. note 84, *infra*, section 4. Advertisement of the Board of Treasury for the sale.

[81] An entry in the Journal of John Matthews (Hildreth's Pioneer History of the Ohio Valley, p. 188) is especially interesting in this connection:
November 30, [1787] A part of this month I have been on the West side of the Ohio with Mr Simpson and Colonel Martin, assisting them in the survey of the lands they bought at the public sales in New York...
There is no record of a sale in the name of Simpson. James Simpson was Surveyor for the State of Maryland in the Geographer's Department, but Capt. Absalom Martin, Surveyor for the State of New Jersey, purchased and occupied as his permanent home two fractional lots on the Ohio River bottoms opposite Wheeling; land which he had himself surveyed under Hutchins the year before. He took possession of his property within a month or six weeks of the date of sale, and appears to be the first known settler in the Western Territory. Captain Martin was the son of Ephraim Martin of Baskenridge, N. J. (cf. Papers of the Continental Congress, No. 56, p. 173), and his place on the Ohio River was the landing place from Wheeling, now known as Martin's Ferry, Ohio.

[82] Many pages of this volume were not used, as the form was changed for the Pittsburgh sale, and only 111 patents were issued. Some of the pages are signed with the names of the three members of the Board of Treasury, but most of them are not so signed. The patents are recorded in the several county records of Ohio, and they correspond with the form given in the Ordinance of May 20, 1785.

of the townships as surveyed, on which are lines drawn at right angles to represent the 36 square lots in each township. The plats are drawn on the scale of 40 chains to the inch, making each of these lots two inches square, on which is written the name of purchaser, date, acres, etc. The lots are numbered, also the townships and ranges as required by the ordinance: Ranges; westward from I to VII beginning with the Pennsylvania line. Townships, northward from the river, each range beginning with Township No. 1, and the lots; northward from the base line of the township, in ranges of six, beginning with Lot I at the southeast corner.[83]

From this data not only the names of owners but the situation of each lot, according to present day geography, may be ascertained[84] and designated by modern names of political divisions, county and township. The region covered by the seven Ranges of Townships may readily be traced on a map

---

[83] Lots or sections in the Seven Ranges of Townships are not numbered as in the later surveys. According to the terms of the ordinance of May 20, 1785:

The plats of the townships respectively shall be marked by subdivisions into lots of one mile square or 640 acres, in the same direction as the external lines and numbered from 1 to 36, always beginning the succeeding range of the lots with the number next to that with which the preceding one concluded,

while the law of May 18, 1796, required that

the sections shall be numbered respectively, beginning with number one, in the northeast section, and proceeding west and east alternately, through the township, with progressive numbers till the thirty-sixth be completed.

Thus it happens that some of the townships of Columbiana, Carroll, and Stark counties, part of which were outside the Old Seven Ranges of Townships, have two sets of townships and sections in the same townships with the same numbers.

[84] The townships offered for sale were described by numerals in the advertisement published by the Board of Treasury, which reads as follows:

TREASURY OF THE UNITED STATES.
May 14, 1787.

THE Commissioners of the Board of Treasury of the United States, give notice, That on the 21st day of September next, will be exposed to Sale, at the place where the United States in Congress may hold their sessions—The following Townships and Lots of Lands in the Western Territory, which were surveyed last year, under the direction of the Geographer General of the United States viz.

First Range.	Third Range.	Fourth Range.
No. 3, containing 4,350 acres.	No. 1, containing 6,596 acres.	No. 1, containing 4,574 acres.
	2, 11,797	2, 21,350
Second Range.	3, 14,482	3, 23,040
No. 1, containing 1,386	5, 23,040	7, 23,040
2, 5,434	6, 23,040	8, 23,040
3, 8,598	7, 23,040	10, 23,040
5, 21,139	8, 23,040	11, 23,040
6, 23,040	9, 23,040	12, 23,040
7, 23,040	10, 23,040	13, 23,040
8, 22,886	11, 23,040	
9, 18,644½	12, 23,040	

The admirable quality of these Lands, and the favorable climate in which they are situated, are too well known to need description. The conditions of sale are as follows, viz.

1st. The townships or fractional parts of townships throughout the different ranges, will be sold either entire or in lots in alternate order; that is to say, where a township or fractional part of a township is sold entire, the next will be sold in lots, agreeably to the ordinance of the 20th of May, 1785.

2d. The lands are not to be sold under a dollar per acre, payable in gold or silver, or any of the securities of the United States.

3d. The purchasers are to pay the charges of survey, which are to be estimated at thirty-six dollars in specie, or certificates as aforesaid for every township; and in the same proportion for fractional parts of townships or lots; this payment to be made at the sales, and in case of failure, the lands to be again exposed to public auction.

4th. One third of the purchase money is to be paid at the time of purchase; and the remaining two thirds in three months after the date of the sale; on which payment a certificate shall be given by the Treasurer of the United States, which shall entitle the person to whom the same is given to receive from the Commissioners of this Board a proper title; provided, that if the second payment is not made at the time above specified, the first payment is to be forfeited, and the land on which the forfeit accrued be again set up for sale.

of Ohio[85] by following the East and West line from the intersection of the Pennsylvania western boundary and the Ohio River westward across seven ranges to the northwest corner of Rose Township, Carroll County (Tp. No. 16),[86] and thence by a meridian line southward across Tuscarawas, Guernsey, Noble, and Washington counties to a point where the meridian crosses the Ohio River about a mile east of the city of Marietta, which is in Township 2 of Range VIII.[87] The lots purchased at the New York sale are all within the four counties, Columbiana, Jefferson, Monroe, and Belmont, and the initials of these counties are used in the following list to indicate the situation of the several lots—closer designations being expressed by names of township, or otherwise.

Arnold H(enry) Dohrman[88]   n p (no patents issued)

5th. The platts of the townships will be marked by subdivisions into lots of one mile square, or 640 acres, and numbered from 1 to 36; and out of each township, Lot No. 8, 11, 26 and 29, are to be reserved for future sale; Lot No. 16, for the maintenance of Public Schools within the respective township, as many lots of the same number as shall be found therein. There will also be reserved to the United States one third part of all gold and silver, lead and copper mines.

Proper maps and descriptions of the lands will be exhibited at the time and place of sale, and the sales will continue from day to day until the whole are sold.

SAMUEL OSGOOD,
WALTER LIVINGSTON, } Commissioners.
ARTHUR LEE,

From
The New York Packet, No. 697, Tuesday, May 15, 1787; Providence Gazette, Aug. 11, 18, 25, Sept. 1, 1787; Connecticut Courant, June 25, July 9, 23, Aug. 6, 1787; Pennsylvania Packet, Sept. 6, 13, 18, 1787; etc., etc.

[85] The latest map of Ohio, issued by the General Land Office, bears the date 1910.

[86] There are two Townships No. 16 in Carroll County, the northernmost being outside the Seven Ranges of Townships.

[87] The Seven Ranges of Townships are first shown on the map entitled:

A Map of the Federal Territory from the Western Boundary of Pennsylvania to the Scioto River, laid down from the latest informations and divided into Townships and fractional parts of Townships agreeably to the ordinance of the Honble Congress passed in May, 1785,

which, according to the Phillips List of Maps of America, p. 626, is the "Map to accompany Cutler's 'Explanation of the map of the federal lands, confirmed by the treaties of 1784...Salem, 1787.'" The famous map issued by Joel Barlow for European exploitation of the Scioto Company's lands, entitled: "Plan des achates des Compagnies de l' Ohio" (Cf. Winsor, vol. vii, p. 532; the Library of Congress has a fine copy of the Barlow map recently picked up by Mr. Phillips in Paris), shows the region marked: "Sept ranges de Municipalitère acquis par des individus, et occupés depuis 1786," and described as "Habité et défriché," which, considering the date of Barlow's activity, 1788, is surprising.

A "Plat of the Seven Ranges of Townships being part of the Territory of the United States N. W. of the River Ohio which by late act of Congress are directed to be sold... W. Barker, Sculp." issued for use of the second sale of lots, shows the survey as altered to fit the latest land laws, 1796. The sub-divisions sold at the New York sale are marked on this plat. This plate seems to have been used by Matthew Carey for editions of the American Atlas as late as 1818. (A reproduction from an original print is in Avery's History, vol. vi, betw. pp. 406 and 407.)

An outline map of the State of Ohio, showing the land divisions, prepared by Col. Chas. Whittlesey and published in W. R. H. S. Tract No. 61, represents the Seven Ranges of Townships as extending northerly to the base line of the Western Reserve, whereas the writings of Col. Whittlesey on this subject, in this and other publications, correctly describe the Ohio surveys. The strip of land, twenty-five miles wide, between the Seven Ranges of Townships and the Western Reserve, was surveyed in 1801 by extending the ranges northward from the East and West line to the 41° of latitude, which was forbidden by earlier resolution of Congress, May 9, 1786.

[88] Dohrman [Dorhman] is the Portuguese refugee honored by Congress (Land Laws of the U. S., p. 222) with liberal pensions in recognition of his services to American sailors during the war. After his escape from Lisbon he appears as a merchant in Chambers Street, New York. No doubt he attended the sale and made the first purchase of land on the public domain. Congress voted to him a township of land in the Seven Ranges of Townships, and he went west to take possession of his property. He lived and died at Steubenville, Jefferson County, where he lies buried, and where his descendants still reside. There are many traditions in the family concerning

II	3	17	1½ acres	1 : 48 dollars[89]	B	Martin's Ferry
II	5	3	48½ "	348 : 67 "	J	Warren Tp.
Absalom Martin				Patents 2–3		March 5. 1783
II	3	18	36½ acres	356 : 73 dollars	B	Martin's Ferry
II	3	23	293¾ "	1321 : 79 "	B	" "
Abijah Hammond				Patents 13–17		March 10, 1788
II	3	19	20½ acres	103 : 70 dollars	B	Pultney Tp.
II	3	20	85 "	340 "	B	" "
II	3	21	4 "	18 : 45 "	B	" "
II	5	1	1½ "	22 : 87 "	J	Warren Tp.
II	5	3	188½ "	836 : 42 "	J	Wells Tp.
Robert Kirkwood (Kerchwood)[90]				Patents 59–62		May 27, 1788
II	3	27	546¾ acres	2204 : 8 dollars	B	Bridgport
II	5	9	640 "	680 "	J	Wells Tp.
II	5	15	640 "	640 "	J	" "
II	5	18	640 "	640 "	J	" "
Jnº Cowenhoven (Covenhoven) Jun				Patents 67–68		July 26, 1788
II	5	4	558½ acres	1083 : 9 dollars	J	Wells Tp.
II	57	7	640 "	640 "	J	Isld Creek Tp.
Wm. McKennan				Patents 67–58		April 27, 1788
II	5	10	640 acres	720 dollars	J	Wells Tp.
II	5	17	640 "	640 "	J	" "
Wm. Manning				Patent 30		April 10, 1788
II	5	13	640 acres	706 : 60 dollars	J	Warren Tp.
John Foulks				Patents 34–36		April 10, 1788
[91]II	5	12	640 acres	720 dollars	J	Wells Tp.
[91]II	9	1	144 "	153 "	J	Saline Tp.
II	9	9	270 "	270 : 68 "	C	Yellow Creek Tp.
III	2	10	75¼ "	228 : 10 "	M	Salem Tp.
Benj. Manning				Patent 33		April 10, 1788
II	5	14	640 acres	660 dollars	J	Warren Tp.
Jacob Martin				Patent 31		April 10, 1788
II	5	19	640 acres	640 dollars	J	Warren Tp.
John Learmonth (Learmouth)				Patents 63–64		May 27, 1788
II	5	20	640 acres	640 dollars	J	Wells Tp.
II	5	21	640 "	640 "	J	" "
John Lyon				Patent 65		May 27, 1788
II	5	22	640 acres	640 dollars	J	Wells Tp.
Honble. Arthur Lee Esq				Patents 8–12		March 10, 1788
II	[92]5	30	640 acres	640 dollars	J	Wells Tp.

their ancestor. Among others is this, that he was taken to Lisbon when an infant by his parents, Dutch adventurers, and was in that fateful city when the earthquake occurred. He was saved from destruction by his nurse, who crawled, with the infant at her breast, under the stone stoop of the house, which shielded him from the flying debris.

[89] Old style notation with fractions in the 90th denomination.

[90] Thus spelled in Record of Patents.

[91] The items are marked Patents 34 and 33 respectively, although they come in the above order.

[92] This patent is entered erroneously as Tp. 3 in Record of Patents.

	II	3	30	640	acres	640	dollars	B	Pease Tp.
	II	3	34	640	"	640	"	B	" "
	II	3	35	640	"	640	"	B	" "
	II	3	36	640	"	640	"	B	" "

James Gray Patents 21–25 March 31, 1788

	II	7	1	640	acres	640	dollars	J	Isl^d Creek Tp.
[93]npII	7	2	640	"	641	"	J	" " "	
	II	7	4	640	"	640	"	J	" " "
	II	7	6	640	"	640	"	J	" " "
	II	7	27	640	"	640	"	J	" " "
[94]npII	7	31	640	"	640	"	J	" " "	
[94]npII	7	32	640	"	640	"	J	" " "	
[94]npII	9	7	639½	"	639 : 45	"	J	Saline Tp.	
	III	2	17	149	"	474 : 85	"	M	Salem Tp.

Daniel Turner Patent 72 September 15, 1788

	II	7	5	640	acres	740	dollars	J	Isl^d Creek Tp.

Doctr. Robt. Johnston (Johnson) Patents 37–55 April 17, 1788

	II	5	31	640	acres	940	dollars	J	Warren Tp.
	II	7	10	640	"	640	"	J	Isl^d Creek Tp.
	II	7	17	640	"	640	"	J	" " "
	II	7	18	640	"	640	"	J	" " "
	II	7	13	640	"	760	"	J	" " "
	II	7	19	640	"	680	"	J	" " "
	II	7	21	640	"	640	"	J	" " "
	II	7	22	640	"	640	"	J	" " "
	II	7	23	640	"	640	"	J	" " "
	II	7	24	640	"	640	"	J	" " "
[95]II	9	4	145¾	"	286 : 85	"	C	Wellsville	
[95]II	7	34	640	"	726 : 60	"	J	Isl^d Creek Tp.	
	II	9	5	542½	"	542 : 45	"	C	Wellsville
	III	6	13	640	"	640	"	B	Pultney Tp.
	III	6	23	640	"	640	"	B	" "
	III	6	24	640	"	640	"	B	" "
	III	8	1	640	"	640	"	J	Smithfield Tp.
	III	10	3	640	"	640	"	J	Salem Tp.
	IV	1	33	221	"	1105	"	M	Cochransville.

John D. Mercier Patent 56 April 23, 1788

	II	7	12	640	acres	720	dollars	J	Isl^d Creek Tp.

Joshua Merereau (Mersereau) Patents 69–71 September 5, 1788

	II	7	28	640	acres	640	dollars	J	Isl^d Creek Tp.
	II	9	10	640	"	640	"	C	Wellsville
	II	9	17	640	"	640	"	C	Yellow Creek Tp.

George Douglass Patent 19 March 20, 1788

	III	2	9	212¼ acres	578 : 53 dollars	M	Ohio Tp.

Henry W. Livingston n p

	III	1	–	5316 acres	5316 dollars	M	Lee Tp.

[93] Patented April 1, 1789, No. 29, to John Crawford.
[94] Patented March 31, 1789, No. 26–28, to William Bowne.
[95] These items are marked Patents 48 and 47 respectively, although they come in the above order.

Cornelius Ray			Patent 18			March 12, 1788	
III	2	19	385¼ acres	385 : 23 dollars		M	Ohio Tp.
James Burnside			Patent 20			March 20, 1788	
III	2	24	240¾ acres	278 : 33 dollars		M	Salem Tp.
Henry Kuhl			Patents 5–7			March 6, 1788	
III	6	3	640 acres	660	dollars	B	Pease Tp.
IV	7	3	640 "	640	"	B	Richland Tp.
IV	7	17	640 "	640	"	B	" "
The Rev. Willm. Linn			Patent 4			March 5, 1788	
III	10	4	640 acres	640	dollars	J	Salem Tp.
Jacob Blackwell			Patent 66			July 26, 1788	
IV	7	10	640 acres	640	dollars	B	Richland Tp.
John Martin			Patent 1			March 4, 1788	
IV	7	20	640 acres	640	dollars	B	Richland Tp.
Alex^r. McComb (Macomb) & Willm. Edgar[96] n p							
II	3	24	640 acres	1280	dollars	B	Martin's Ferry
II	3	26	640 "	800	"	B	Pultney Tp.
II	3	29	640 "	640	"	B	Pease Tp.
II	3	31	640 "	640	"	B	Mead Tp.
II	3	32	640 "	640	"	B	" "
II	5	5	640 "	1326 : 60	"	J	Wells Tp.
II	5	6	640 "	1306 : 60	"	J	" "
II	5	7	640 "	1600	"	J	Warren Tp.
II	5	23	640 "	640	"	J	Wells Tp.
II	5	24	640 "	640	"	J	" "
II	5	25	640 "	640	"	J	Warren Tp.
II	5	27	640 "	640	dollars	J	Wells Tp.
II	5	28	640 "	640	"	J	" "
II	5	32	640 "	640	"	J	Warren Tp.
II	5	33	640 "	640	"	J	Wells Tp.
II	5	34	640 "	640	"	J	" "
II	5	35	640 "	640	"	J	" "
II	5	36	640 "	960	"	J	" "
II	6	–[97]	19840 "	19840	"	J	Cross Creek Tp.
II	7	3	640 "	640	"	J	Isl^d Creek Tp.
II	8	–[97]	19686 "	19686	"	J	Knox and Saline
II	9	13	640 "	640	"	J	Saline Tp. [Tp.

[96] Alexander Macomb and William Edgar, of the city of New York, memorialized Congress, praying
that they may be permitted to complete the payment of the purchase money of a quantity of land, in the territory of the United States, northwest of the river Ohio, on the original terms of the purchase, and to obtain a grant for the same; or, that a law may be passed for granting to the memorialists so much of the said land, as will be in proportion which the sum heretofore paid by them bears to the whole amount of the purchase money.
The memorial was read in the House, May 13, 1796 (Journal of the House, 4th Congress, 1st Session, p. 435), and reported upon by the committee on claims, January 30, 1798 (5th Cong. 2d Sess., p. 179), and on the 30th of April following (p. 438–439) it was resolved in the affirmative to agree with the report, which was in part as follows:

Several of the lots for which the petitioners made their contract having been sold at Pittsburgh, in pursuance of the act of the eighteenth of May, one thousand seven hundred and ninety-six, if the prayer of the petition should be granted, it will be necessary to indemnify the petitioners, by granting other lots of equivalent value.
But, as the petitioners have shown no reason why they did not proceed to fulfil their contract, excepting that their funds were otherwise employed, and as the United States must have incurred considerable expenses in the negotiation when the contract was made with the petitioners, the committee can find no reason why the forfeiture to which the petitioners have subjected themselves by the terms of their contract, should be remitted. They therefore report, as their opinion, that the prayer of the petition ought not to be granted."

	II	9	14	640 acres	640 dollars	J	"	"
	II	9	19	640 "	640 "	J	"	"
	II	9	20	640 "	640 "	J	"	"
	III	6	18	640 "	640 "	B	Colerain Tp.	
	III	6	30	640 "	653:31 "	B	"	"
	III	6	36	640 "	640 "	B	"	"
	III	8	6	640 "	640 "	J	Smithfield Tp.	
	IV	1	24	640 "	1380 "	M	Jackson Tp.	
	IV	1	34	636 "	1590 "	M	"	"
	III	7	—[97]	19840 "	25420 "	B and J	Colerain and Mt. Pleasant Tps.	

Nathan McFarland   Patents 107 and 110   March 3, 1789
(Patented except 107 and 110 to Richard Platt)

np	II	7	9	640 acres	640 dollars	J	Isl^d Creek Tp.	
np	II	7	15	640 "	640 "	J	"	" "
np	II	7	14	640 "	680 "	J	"	" "
np	II	7	20	640 "	640 "	J	"	" "
np	II	7	25	640 "	726:60 "	J	"	" "
np	II	7	30	640 "	640 "	J	"	" "
np	II	7	35	640 "	640 "	J	"	" "
np	II	7	36	640 "	640 "	J	"	" "
np	II	9	12	640 "	640 "	C	Yellow Creek Tp.	
np	II	9	18	640 "	640 "	C	"	" "
np	III	2	14	106½ "	342:73 "	M	Ohio Tp.	
np	III	6	1	640 "	640 "	B	Pultney Tp.	
np	III	6	2	640 "	640 "	B	"	"
np	III	6	4	640 "	640 "	B	Pease Tp.	
np	III	6	5	640 "	640 "	B	"	"
	III	6	7	640 "	640 "	B	Pultney Tp.	
np	III	8	2	640 "	640 "	J	Smithfield Tp.	
np	III	8	24	640 "	640 "	J	"	"
	IV	1	23	333 "	1332 "	M	Jackson Tp.	
np	IV	1	28	208½ "	873:8 "	M	"	"

John Hopkins   Patents 73–82   March 3, 1789

np	I	3	—	3340 acres	4488:11 dollars	J	Isl^d Creek Tp.	
	II	1	29	247¾ "	929:6 "	B	Mead Tp.	
	II	1	30	86⅔ "	351:36 "	B	"	"
	II	1	35	413¼ "	619:79 "	B	"	"
np	II	2	—	4154 "	5365:53 "	B	Pultney Tp.	
	IV	7	15	640 "	640 "	B	Richland Tp.	
	IV	7	21	640 "	640 "	B	"	" "
	IV	7	22	640 "	640 "	B	"	" "
	IV	7	23	640 "	640 "	B	"	" "
	IV	7	24	640 "	640 "	B	"	" "
	IV	7	27	640 "	640 "	B	"	" "
	IV	7	28	640 "	640 "	B	"	" "

Willm. Duer, Esqr.   Patents 83–88   March 3, 1789

	II	1	36	640 acres	646:60 dollars	B	Mead Tp.
	II	7	33	640 "	1313:31 "	J	Isl^d Creek Tp.
	III	8	31	640 "	640 "	J	Smithfield Tp.
	IV	7	4	640 "	640 "	B	St. Clairsville

[97] Entire townships minus the reservations.

IV	7	9	640	acres	640	dollars	B	Richland Tp.
IV	7	14	640	"	640	"	B	" "

Joseph Hardy   Patents 89–91   March 3, 1789

III	6	6	640	acres	640	dollars	B	Pease Tp.
III	8	32	640	"	640	"	J	Smithfield Tp.
IV	1	18	149½	"	373 : 68	"	M	Jackson Tp.

Willm. Bowne[98]   Patents 26–28   March 31, 1789
(Entered in Schedule of Sales under the name of James Gray purchaser)

II	7	31	640	acres	640	dollars	J	Isl^d Creek Tp.
II	7	32	640	"	780	"	J	" " "
II	9	7	659½	"	639 : 45	"	C	Saline Tp.

John Crawford[98]   Patent 29   April 1, 1789
(Entered in Schedule of Sales under the name of James Gray purchaser)

II	7	2	640	acres	640	dollars	J	Isl^d Creek Tp.

Richard Platt[98] Patents 92–111 (except 107 & 110)   March 3, 1789
(Entered in Schedule of Sales under the name of Nathan McFarland purchaser)

II	7	9	640	acres	640	dollars	J	Isl^d Creek Tp.
II	7	15	640	"	640	"	J	" " "
II	7	14	640	"	680	"	J	" " "
II	7	20	640	"	640	"	J	" " "
II	7	25	640	"	726 : 60	"	J	" " "
II	7	30	640	"	640	"	J	" " "
II	7	35	640	"	640	"	J	" " "
II	7	36	640	"	640	"	J	" " "
II	9	12	640	"	640	"	C	Yellow Creek Tp.
II	9	18	640	"	640	"	C	" " "
III	2	14	106½	"	342 : 72	"	M	Ohio Tp.
III	6	1	640	"	640	"	B	Pultney Tp.
III	6	2	640	"	640	"	B	" "
III	6	4	640	"	640	"	B	Pease Tp.
III	6	5	640	"	640	"	B	" "
III	8	2	640	"	640	"	J	Smithfield Tp.
III	8	24	640	"	640	"	J	" "
IV	1	28	208½	"	873 : 8	"	M	Jackson Tp.

Land Owners on the Muskingum

While the first sale of lots was in progress at New York, the agents and directors of the Ohio Company of Associates were negotiating with the Committee of Congress for the purchase of the tract of land on the Muskingum River, west of the seventh range of townships. Papers were signed for this purchase, and for the Scioto River tract, on the 27th of October, 1787, and title to the property passed from the United States on that date. Prior to this date the Ohio Company had arranged to apportion the lands of their purchase among the proprietor-shareholders of the company, in number about a thousand, one numbered subdivision in each allotment for each share. Plans were formed at a series of meetings, beginning August 29, 1787, and extending beyond the date of signature to July 7, 1788, for the distribution of these shares of the lands to the proprietors by a method of drafts, the details of which appear in the form of resolutions

---

[98] These names: William Bowne, John Crawford, and Richard Platt do not appear in the Schedule of Sales.

entered in the manuscript minutes of the Ohio company.[99]

[99] The minutes of the Ohio Company of Associates are in the Library of Marietta College, Marietta, Ohio. Extracts covering the matter of the drafts may be found in a set of four page leaflets issued, without date or title, for purposes of advancing the sale of shares in the company. A set of these leaflets is in the Col. John May Collection, W. R. H. S., attached to Col. May's copy of Dr. Cutler's famous pamphlet "An Explanation of the Map which Delineates that part of the Federal Lands . . ." Salem, 1787. References to the subdivisions of the lands and the process of drafts as actually carried out, taken from these sources, follow:

(The instructions of August 30, respecting the allotments, which appear in the *Massachusetts Gazette*, Tuesday, September 11, 1787, were never carried out, but were displaced by later regulations.—A. M. D.)

At a Meeting of the DIRECTORS *and* AGENTS *of the* Ohio Company, at Mr. Brackett's *Tavern, the 21st. of November, and continued by Adjournment to the twenty-second.*

RESOLVED,

That the lands of the Ohio Company be allotted and divided in the following manner; anything to the contrary, in former resolutions notwithstanding—Viz.

Four thousand acres near the confluence of the Ohio and Muskingum river for a city and commons, and contiguous to *this*, one thousand lots of eight acres each, amounting to eight thousand acres.

Upon the Ohio in fractional townships, one thousand lots of one hundred and sixteen and 48/100, amounting to one hundred and sixteen thousand four hundred and eighty acres.

In the townships on the navigable rivers, one thousand lots of three hundred and twenty acres, amounting to three hundred and twenty thousand acres, AND,

In the inland towns, one thousand lots of nine hundred and ninety two acres each, amounting to nine hundred and ninety two thousand acres, to be divided and allotted as the agents shall hereafter direct.

RESOLVED, that the city at the mouth of the Muskingum river be so laid out into oblong squares, as that each house-lot shall consist of ninety feet in front, and one hundred and eighty feet in depth, with an alley of ten feet in width, through each square in its oblong direction; and that the centre street, crossing the city, be one hundred and fifty feet wide, anything to the contrary, in former resolutions, notwithstanding.

RESOLVED, That the eight acre lots be surveyed, and a plat or map thereof be made, with each lot numbered thereon, by the first Wednesday in March next, and that a copy thereof, be immediately forwarded to the Secretary, and the original retained by the Company's Superintendant. That the Agents meet upon the same Wednesday in March, at *Rice's* Tavern in Providence, State of Rhode-Island, to draw for said lots in numbers, as the same shall be stated upon the plat. That a list of the draughts be transmitted by the Secretary to the Superintendant, and a copy thereof preserved in the Secretary's office.

WINTHROP SARGENT, *Sec'ry to the Ohio Company.*

At a Meeting of the DIRECTORS *of the* Ohio Company *at Mr.* Brackett's *Tavern, in Boston, November* 23, 1787.

For the purpose of carrying into effect the surveys and other business of the Ohio Company; as agreed upon by the Directors, and Agents, at their meetings of the 29th. of August last, and the 21st. instant.

ORDERED,

That Col. *Ebenezer Sproat*, from *Rhode-Island*, Mr. *Anslem Tupper*, and Mr. *John Matthews*, from *Massachusetts*, and Col. *R. J. Meigs*, from *Connecticut*, be the surveyors.

That General *Rufus Putnam*, be the Superintendant of all the business aforesaid, and he is to be obeyed and respected accordingly.

General PARSONS in the Chair.

General Varnum, General Tupper, Mr. Barlow, Col. May, and Capt. Heyward, were appointed a Committee to examine into, and report upon, the returns of the Agents.

This Committee reported, that one thousand shares of the Ohio Company's purchase were taken up by the Agents, and that the drawing for the eight acre lots may commence as soon as the Meeting shall direct; which report was accepted and approved.

RESOLVED, That the Secretary enter upon the records the number of shares in each agency.

RESOLVED, That Mr. Cutler, General Parsons, Major Dexter, Col. Talmadge, and Major Corlis, be a Committee to prepare the names and numbers, and make all necessary arrangements for drawing the eight acre lots.

RESOLVED, That the drawing shall commence tomorrow morning, at the State-House in this town.

Adjourned till tomorrow morning, at 9 o'clock.

Thursday, March 6.

Met agreeably to adjournment.

The committee for preparing names and numbers reported, that they had procured two boxes, into the one of which they had put the names of the adventurers, as returned by the Agents (amounting to one thousand) and into the other the numbers, from No. 1 to No. 1000 inclusive:

That they have procured two lads to assist in drawing out the names and numbers.

That they have appointed Colonel J. May to receive the numbers, and call them off; and Major W. Sargent to receive and call off the names; And,

That they have appointed General H. Jackson, and Col. Talmadge, Clerks; and General B. Tupper to receive and string the several names and numbers together, as they shall be severally drawn out.

RESOLVED—, That the report of the Committee be accepted and approved; and that the Meeting adjourn to the State-House immediately, and proceed to drawing the lots.

Adjourned to the State-House.

At 9 o'clock, P.M. having completed the drawing of the names and numbers (a list of which is with the files of the Company, in the Secretary's office) the Meeting adjourned till to-morrow morning, at 9 o'clock, at Mr. Rice's Tavern.

Lists of the drafts kept by Col. May furnish means of obtaining the names of the proprietors of the Ohio Company, owners of lands on the Muskingum River, 1788–1792.[100] They present the drafts by name and number of the proprietor, the agency from which the shares were obtained, and the various numbers of the lots drawn against each name. An early list, dated 1788, gives names about in order of the alphabet, but a later list, 1796,[101] gives data from which corrections may be made, showing changes of residence, assignments of title, forfeitures, etc. A list, constructed from these sources follows, giving names of proprietors, residence, agency and number of shares held,[102] the corrections taken from the attested copy being inserted in each case in brackets.

Extracts from the Journal of Col. John May (Cincinnati, Robert Clarke & Co., 1873), relating to the distribution of lots on the Muskingum:

p. 59. [May 27, 1788] As to our surveying, buildings, etc., they are in a very backward way. Little appears to be done, and a great deal of time and money misspent. . . .

p. 60. [May 28, 1788] The directors and agents present agreed to lease the *ministerial lot* to different persons, in lots of ten acres each, for a term not less than one hundred years, at the option of the lessee—to be without rent the first ten years, and then a fixed rent the remainder of the time. This was done to accommodate a number of proprietors present, whose *eight-acre lots* were drawn at a distance. Went this afternoon to survey the *ten-acre lots*, and drew for them in the evening. Colonel Sproat drew No. 9; Varnum, 10; May, 11; Sargent, 12; Parsons, 13, etc. . . .

p. 63. [June 7, 1788] General Varnum and his party are making difficulties about the *eight-acre lots* not being drawn contiguous to the city; also, with respect to the Scioto purchase. The rations are not good. General Putnam did not strictly adhere to orders given at Brackett's tavern in Boston, and Rice's tavern at Providence. I think I foresee difficulties of a more serious nature.

p. 65. [June 9, 1788] . . . Met to settle difficulties respecting the eight-acre lots; but we could not agree, and adjourned until to-morrow, at 8 o'clock A.M. . . .

p. 66. [June 10, 1788] . . . Met this morning, according to adjournment, and after much debate and discussion, agreed to cut up our commons into *three-acre* lots, to be drawn for in July. This has appeased the minds of the people. We also appointed officers of police.

p. 76. [July 2, 1788] . . . Attended myself a meeting of directors and agents, according to order at Providence, 8th March. Chose a committee to make preparation for drawing *the city lots*. Entered into several debates, and at 2 o'clock adjourned until Monday, 7th inst., at 8 o'clock in the morning, for the purpose of *drawing the city lots*, and transacting such other business as may be thought necessary for the establishment of our infant settlement. . . .

p. 79. [July 5, 1788] . . . I am employed myself in *preparing for the draughts of the city lots*. . . .

p. 82. [July 7, 1788] . . . We have drawn the city lots to-day. . . .

[100] Several of the official drafts, two of which are in the library of the New England Historic Genealogical Society, were found in the chest of Col. John May, which, with its contents, is now in the Western Reserve Historical Society.

[101] In the Col. John May collection, W. R. H. S. Attested copy of an instrument executed February 1, 1796, whereby agents of the Ohio Company relinquish and quit-claim to each proprietor the allotments made in the several drafts, viz.

one lot of eight acres,
one lot of three acres,
one lot of 100 acres,
one house or town lot, 6th division { one lot of 640 acres,
one lot of 262 acres.
one lot of 160 acres,

[102] The agencies employed in selling shares in the Ohio Company are given by full title in the attested copy of the deed, although appearing in earlier lists by catchword. A list of these agents as entered in the deed, with numbers of shares sold by each, follows:

Agency	Shares	Nos.
Barlow's Agency	19 shares	1– 19 inclusive
William Corlis's Agency	108 "	" 20–127 "
A Crary's Agency	71 "	" 128–198 "
M. Cutler & J Dodge Agency	86 "	" 199–284 "
Ephraim Cutler's Agency	13 "	" 285–297 "
Eliphalet Downer's Agency	18 "	" 298–315 "
N. Freeman's Agency	9 "	" 316–324 "
E. Harris's Agency	31 "	" 325–355 "
H. Jackson's Agency	13 "	" 356–368 "
Jno May's Agency	35 "	" 369–403 "
S. H. Parson's Agency	91 "	" 404–492 and 816–817
R. Putnam & Co. Agency	59 "	" 493–551 inclusive
W. Sargent's Agency	148 "	" 552–699 "
Sproat & Dexter's Agency	43 "	" 700–742 "
Benj[n] Tupper's Agency	30 "	" 743–772 "
Benj[n] Tallmadge's Agency	43 "	" 773–815 "

PROPRIETOR	RESIDENCE	AGENCY	SHARES
Aborn, Samuel	Cranston, R. I. [Warwick]	[William] Corlis	3
" "	Warwick, R. I.	[Sproat &] Dexter	1
Adams, David	Mansfield, Conn.	[S. H.] Parsons	2
" Samuel	Durham, N. H.	[M. Cutler & J. Dodge]	1
Alden, John	Ashfield, Mass.	[Benjn] Tupper	1 [0]¹⁰³
Allen, Elisha	Middleton, R. I.	Crary	1 [0]
Allis, Lucius	Conway, Mass.	Tupper	1
Angel, Israel	Johnston, R. I.	[Sproat &] Dexter	3 [1]
[" " and Windsor, Christ^{er}	" "	" "	1]¹⁰⁴
" " and Mathewson, Jeffery	" "	" "	1
Arnold, Nathan	Providence	[William] Corlis	3
" Stephen	E. Greenwich, R. I. [Greenwich]	[A.] Crary	1
" Welcome	" "	" "	1
" William	Providence	[William] Corlis	4
Ashley, Moses, and [Hill, Asa]	E. Greenwich, R. I. [Greenwich]	[A.] Crary	2
Ashton, Joseph	Stockbridge, Mass.	[Benjn] Tupper	2 [1]
Atkinson, John	Ohio	[W.] Sargent	1
Atwater, Caleb	New York	M. Cutler [& J. Dodge]	3
Atwood, Ebenezer	Wallingford, Conn.	[S. H.] Parsons	1
Babcock, Abijah [Alijah]	Killingly, Conn.	E[phraim] Cutler	1
Backus, [Bachus] Andrew, and [Jones, Jno. P.] his heirs	S. Kingstown, R. I. [Kingstown]	[A.] Crary	1
Backus, James	Plainfield, Conn. [no address]	[S. H.] Parsons	1
Baker, Eleazer	Norwich, Conn.	" "	1
Barlow, Aaron	Brookline, Mass. [Brooklyn]	[Eliphalet] Downer	1
" Jabez	Reading, Conn.	Barlow	5 [0]
" Joel [& Asso:]	Southbury, Conn.	" "	1 [0]
	Hartford, Conn. [Reading]	" "	3

¹⁰³ The numerals in brackets indicate the number of shares entered in the quit-claim deed.
¹⁰⁴ This and other names thus expressed do not appear in the early lists showing a transfer of title.

Barrill [Barrell], Joseph	Boston	M. Cutler [& J. Dodge]	5
Barlet[t], William	Beverly, Mass.	"	1
Barton, William	Providence	[William] Corlis	1
Basset, Barakiah	Falmouth, Mass.	[N.] Freeman	1
Bates, Joseph	Rochester, Mass.	"	1
[Beardslee, John	Stratford		1]
Beatty [Beaty], Ercurias	Ohio [Princetown]	Benj. Tallmadge	3
Beauman, Sabastian	New York	[W.] Sargent	1
Beers, Nathan	New Haven, Conn.	"	1
Bent, Silas	Rutland, Mass.	[S. H.] Parsons	1
Big[ge]llow, Timothy, and [Bent, Silas, &c.]	Worcester, Mass.	Clapp [R. Putnam & Co.]	1
Bird, Seth	Litchfield, Conn.	"	1
Blake, Thomas	Boston	Talmage [Benj. Tallmadge]	1
Blanchard, Augustus	Amherst, N. H.	[Jno.] May	1
Bond, John	Hemstead, N. H. [Hempsted]	M. Cutler [& J. Dodge]	1
Boss, John L.	Newport, R. I.	[E.] Harris	1
Bowdoin, Elizabeth [Eliza.:]	Boston	[A.] Crary	4
" James	"	[W.] Sargent	5
Bowen, Israel	Coventry, R. I.	[Jno.] May	1
" Jabez	Providence	[A.] Crary	2
" Obadiah	"	[William] Corlis	1
" William	"	"	1
Bowers, Henry, Jur.	Cambridge, Mass.	[Eliphalet] Downer	2
" John	Swansey, Mass.	"	1
Bowland [Borland], Leonard N.	Boston	[W.] Sargent	1
Bradford, James [Heirs]	Ohio	"	1
" William	Bristol, R. I.	[William] Corlis	1
Brasher [Brosher], Philander	New York	[W.] Sargent	1
Brazer [Brashier], Samuel, and [Choate, Francis]	Worcester, Mass.	Clapp [R. Putnam & Co.]	1
Breeze [Breese], John	Newport, R. I.	[A.] Crary	2
Brick [Breik], William	Boston	[Jno.] May	1

Briggs, Joseph	Newport, R. I.	[A.] Crary	1
Britt, Daniel	Ohio	[W.] Sargent	1
Broadstreet, Nathaniel	Rowley, Mass.	M. Cutler	1 [0]
Broome [Broom], Samuel	New Haven, Conn.	[S. H.] Parsons	5
Brown, Abigail [alias Francis]	Providence	[William] Corlis	2
" Allice	"	"	2
" Ann	New York	[W.] Sargent	1
" Daniel	Ipswich, Mass.	M. Cutler	1 [0]
" Jacob	Newbury, Mass.	[E.] Harris	1
" James	Providence	[William] Corlis	5
" John	"	"	5
" Moses, Jur., *and* [Nicholas]	"	"	3
" N. James [James, son to Nathl]	Ipswich, Mass.	[A.] Crary	1
" Nathaniel	Providence	M. Cutler [& J. Dodge]	5
" Nicholas	"	[William] Corlis	3
" " Junr., *and* [Nicholas]	"	"	2
" Salley [Sally]	"	[William] Corlis	4
" Sarah	Ipswich, Mass.	M. Cutler	1 [0]
" Stephen	Providence	[A.] Crary	1
" William S.	Rutland, Mass.	Clapp [R. Putnam & Co.]	1
Browning, Willm. Jur.	Hebron, Conn.	[S. H.] Parsons	1
Buel, John H.	Worthington, Mass.	[Benj.] Tupper	1
Buffinton, Samuel	Hartford, Conn.	[S. H.] Parsons	1
Bull, David	Pomfret, Conn.	"	1
Burnham, Isaac	Dunbarton, N. H.	M. Cutler	1 [0]
" John	Ipswich, Mass.	" [& J. Dodge]	3
" "	Lynnfield, Mass. [Ipswich]	Heywood [R. Putnam & Co.]	1
" William	Ipswich, Mass.	M. Cutler [& J. Dodge]	1
Burr, Shubal [Shubael], *and* [Samuel]	Warren, R. I.	[William] Corlis	1
Butler, Jeremiah	Durham, Conn.	[S. H.] Parsons	1

Cady, Squier [Squire]	Plainfield, Conn.	1	E[phraim] Cutler
Caldwell, William, *and* [Goodale, Nathan]	Rutland, Mass.	2	Clapp [R. Putnam & Co.]
Call, Jonathan, [& True, Jabez]	Newburyport, Mass.	1	[E.] Harris
Camp, Elnathan	Durham, Conn.	1	[S. H.] Parsons
Campbell, Alexander	Chester, N. H.	1 [0]	Harris
Caning, Henry	New London, Conn.	1 [0]	M. Cutler
Carpenter, Asahel	Rehoboth, Mass.	1	[William] Corlis
" Thomas	"	1	"
Carrington, Edward	Richmond, Vt.	4	[W.] Sargent
Carter, John	Providence	5 [1]	[William] Corlis
Casey, Wanton	Warwick, R. I.	2	[A.] Crary
Cass, Jonathan	Exeter, N. H.	1	[E.] Harris
Catling [Catlin], Alexander	Litchfield, Conn.	1	Talmage [Benj. Tallmadge]
Center [alias Senter], Isaac	Newport, R. I.	2	[A.] Crary
Champney, Caleb	Boston	1	[W.] Sargent
Chapman, Levi	Saybrook, Conn.	2 [1]	[S. H.] Parsons
[" *and* [Shipman, Sam'l]	"	2 [1]	"
Chevalee, John Agin [Chevallie, John H.]	New York	2	[W.] Sargent
Chever, Joshua	Lynn, Mass.	1 [0]	M. Cutler
" Lott [Lot]	"	1	" [& J. Dodge]
Chickery, Jabez	Dedham, Mass.	1 [0]	"
Child, John	Warrin, R. I. [Warren]	1	[William] Corlis
Choate, Jonathan, *and* [Miles, Benjamin]	Rutland, Mass.	1	Clapp [R. Putnam & Co.]
Clap, Caleb	"	1	"
" Daniel	"	1	"
" Joshua [& Daniel]	"	1	Heywood [R. Putnam & Co.]
Clark, Ethan	Worcester, Mass.	1	"
Clark, Peleg	Hardwick, Mass. [Harwich]	1	[A.] Crary
Cleaveland [Cleveland], Moses	Newport, R. I.	1	[A.] Crary
" William	Newport, R. I.	2	[S. H.] Parsons
Clough, Aaron	Canterbury, Conn.	2	M. Cutler [& J. Dodge]
	Salem, Mass.	1	E[phraim] Cutler
	Thompson, Conn. [Marietta]	1	

Cobb, Benjamin	Boston	[Jno.] May	2
" David		[W.] Sargent	1
Coburn, Asa, [& Asso:]	Ta[u]nton, Mass.	Foster [R. Putnam & Co.]	3
Cogswell, James	Brookfield, Mass.	Parsons	1 [0]
Coit, Joseph	New York	E. Cutler	1 [0]
" Wheeler C. [Wheeler.]	Thompson, Conn.	[S. H.] Parsons	1
Coldin, Henritte [Colden, Henrietta]	Preston, Conn.	[W.] Sargent	5
Coles, Thomas	New York	[Sproat &] Dexter	1
Colton, Abijah	Providence	Barlow	1
Comstock, Benjamin	Hartford, Conn.	[William] Corlis	1
Conant, Nathaniel	Sanford, Mass.	M. Cutler	1 [0]
Condy [Candy], Thos. Hollis [H.]	Boston	[W.] Sargent	1
Congdon, James	Charleston, R. I.	[A.] Crary	1
Constable, William	New York	[W.] Sargent	5
Converse, Alpheus	Thompson, Conn.	E[phraim] Cutler	2
" Benjamin, and [James & heirs]	Killingly [Thompson], Conn.	"	1
Cook, Stephen	Watertown, Mass.	[Eliphalet] Downer	1
Cooper, Ezekiel [& Putnam, Jethro]	Danvers[e], Mass.	M. Cutler [& J. Dodge]	1 [1]
Corlis, George, and [Bowen, William]	Providence	[William] Corlis	1 [1]
" and [Nightingale, Joseph]	"	"	1 [1]
" and [Sessions, William]	"	"	3
" William, and [John]	"	"	2
Cory, Ebenezer	Tiverton, R. I.	Crary	1 [0]
Crary, Archibald	E. Greenwich	"	1 [0]
[" " and King, Saml.	"	A. Crary	5
[" " and Martin, Simeon	"	"	1 1
Crook, John	Newport	[A] Crary	1 [0]
" William	"	"	1
Crosby, Ebenezer	New York	[W.] Sargent	1
Crowley, Florence	Boston	"	1
Cummings, Joseph	Topsfield, Mass.	M. Cutler	2 [0]

Name	Location	Agent	Shares
Currier, Samuel	Hamstead [Hempsted], N. H.	[E.] Harris	1
Cushing, Nathaniel [& Asso:]	Brookfield, Mass.	Foster [R. Putnam & Co.]	1
" Thomas	Salem, Mass.	M. Cutler	1 [0]
Cutler, Ephraim [to Moulton, Joseph]	Killingly, Conn. [Marietta][105]	[& J.] Dodge	2
" Manassah	Ipswich, Mass.	[M. Cutler & J.] Dodge	5
Dall, William	Boston	[Jno.] May	1
Davis, Daniel	Killingly, Conn.	E[phraim] Cutler	1
[" Perah	E. Hampton	Benj. Tallmadge	1]
Day, Joseph [& Asso:]	Hartford, Conn.	Barlow	1
Dean, Elizabeth	Dedham, Mass.	M. Cutler	1 [0]
" [Deane], Nathaniel, Jur.	"	" [& J. Dodge]	1
" Thomas	Ipswich, Mass.	" " [& J. Dodge]	1 [0]
Deane [Dean], Jonathan	Dedham, Mass.	" " [& J. Dodge]	5 [2]
" Samuel H.	"	" " [& J. Dodge]	1 [0]
Deavenport [Davenport], James	Stanford [Stamford], Conn.	[S. H.] Parsons	1
Delafield, John	New York	[W.] Sargent	5
Deming, Jonathan [to Deshon, John]	Colchester [N. London], Conn.	[S. H.] Parsons	1 [0]
Demrick, Joseph	Falmouth, Mass.	Freeman	1
Demount, Mary, *and* [Rebecka]	Providence	[William] Corlis	1
Denney [Denny], Ebenezer	Ohio	[W.] Sargent	1
DeNeufville, Leonard	New York	"	2
Deshon, John	New London, Conn.	[S. H.] Parsons	1
Devenport [Davenport], John, *and* [Jones, J. P. and his heirs]	Stamford, Conn. [*no address*]	"	1
Devol, Jonathan	Tiverton, R. I. [Marietta]	[A.] Crary	2 [1]
Dexter, John S.	Cumberland, R. I.	[Sproat &] Dexter	4
" Sam'l S. [L.]	Newburyport	[E.] Harris	1
" Timothy			5
Dewolf, Charles	Bristol, R. I.	[William] Corlis	1

[105] Indicating removal to the Muskingum.

Name	Place	Agent	Count	[?]
Dix, Elijah	Worcester, Mass.	Heywood [R. Putnam & Co.]	2	[0]
Dodge, Isaac [& Oliver]	Wenham, Mass. [Hampton]	[M. Cutler & J.] Dodge	1	
" John	Beverly, Mass.	"	2	[0]
" " Jur.	Wenham, Mass.	Dodge	2	[0]
" John Thornton	"	"	1	[0]
" Oliver	"	"	1	[0]
" Richard, *and* [Woodbury, Nathan]	Hampton, N. H.	"	5	[0]
" William	Wenham, Mass. [Hampton]	[M. Cutler & J.] Dodge	1	
Dolliver, Peter	Boston	M. Cutler	1	[0]
Donalson, James	London Derry, N. H.	Harris	1	[0]
Dorr, Ebenezer	Boston	[Jno.] May	1	[0]
Dorrance, Samuel	Saybrook, Conn.	[S. H.] Parsons	1	
Doughty, John	Ohio	[W.] Sargent	2	[1]
" " *and* [Kerr, Hamilton]	"	"		[1]
Douglas, Richard	New London, Conn.	[S. H.] Parsons	1	
Downer, Eliphalet	Brookline, Mass. [Roxbury]	[Eliphalet] Downer	2	[0]
Dreson, Jacob	Thompson, Conn.	E. Cutler	1	
Drowne [Drown], Solomon	Providence	[Sproat &] Dexter	1	[0]
Duer, William	New York	Sargent	5	[0]
Duglas [Douglas], John	Plainfield, Conn.	Parsons [Ephraim Cutler]	1	
Dunham, Daniel [Danl's heirs]	Conway, Mass.	[Benjⁿ.] Tupper	1	[0]
Dustin, Amos	Salem, Mass.	M. Cutler	1	
Dyar [Dyer], Eliphalet	Windham, Conn.	[S. H.] Parsons	1	[0]
Easton, Nichols [Nichl^s]	Middleton, R. I.	[A.] Crary	1	
Edgar, William	New York	[W.] Sargent	2	
Ensworth, Jedediah	Pomfret, Conn.	[William] Corlis	5	
Evans, Israel	Charlesto[w]n, Mass.	[W.] Sargent	1	
Everett, Moses	Dorchester, Mass.	M. Cutler [& J. Dodge]	2	[0]
Fairchild, Major	Newport	[A] Crary	1	
Farley, Thomas	Ipswich, Mass.	M. Cutler	1	[0]

Name	Place	Agent		
Far[e]well, Isaac	Charlesto[w]n, N. H.	Foster [R. Putnam & Co.]	1	[0]
Fearing, Paul	Middleborough, Mass.	Freeman	1	[0]
"	" [Marietta]	Heywood [R. Putnam & Co.]	1	[0]
Felshaw, John	Killingly, Conn.	Harris	1	
Fisk, Caleb	Scituate, R. I.	[Sproat &] Dexter	2	
" Peleg	"	"	1	
Fitch, Andrew	Lebanon, Conn.	[S. H.] Parsons	1	
Flagg, Samuel	Worcester, Mass.	Heywood [R. Putnam & Co.]	1	[0]
Flint, Hesekiah	Reading, Mass.	M. Cutler	1	
Fogg, Jeremiah	Kensington [Kingston], N. H.	[E.] Harris	1	[0]
Forbes, Eli	Gloucester	M. Cutler	1	
Foster, Dwight	Brookfield, Mass.	Heywood [R. Putnam & Co.]	1	[0]
" Gedion	Danverse, Mass.	M. Cutler	1	
" Peregrine	Brookfield, Mass. [Worcester]	Foster [R. Putnam & Co.]	1	[0]
Fox, Reuben	Warren, Conn.	Talmage [Benj. Tallmadge]	1	
Foster, Theodore	Providence	[Sproat &] Dexter	1	
Fulham, John	E. Greenwich, R. I.	[A.] Crary	1	
Fuller, Daniel	Gloucester	M. Cutler [& J. Dodge]	1	
" Oliver	Rehoboth	[Sproat &] Dexter	1	
Furnice [Furnace], Nathaniel H.	Boston	[Eliphalet] Downer	1	
Fra[u]ncis, Andrew	New York	[W.] Sargent	1	
Freeman, Nathaniel	Sandwich, Mass.	Freeman	1	[0]
Friend, John	Wenham, Mass. [Dorchester]	M. Cutler [& J. Dodge]	4	[1]
Frost, Samuel	Framingham, Mass.	Heywood [R. Putnam & Co.]	1	
Frothingham, Ebenezer	Middleton, Conn.	[S. H.] Parsons	1	
" Samuel	"	"	1	
Frye [Fry], Frederick	Andover, Mass.	Clapp [R. Putnam & Co.]	1	[0]
Gardner, Benjamin	Marblehead, Mass.	M. Cutler	1	
" Caleb	Newport, R. I.	[A.] Crary	2	
[Gardiner, David	E. Hampton	[Benjⁿ] Tallmadge	2]	
Gay, Jesse	Dedham, Mass.	M. Cutler [& J. Dodge]	1	

Name	Address	Agent	Shares
Gerrey [Gerry], Elbridge	Cambridge, Mass.	[Jno.] May	1
Gibbs, George	Newport, R. I.	[A.] Crary	1
Gilman, Benja. T. [Benja. I.]	Exeter, N. H. [Marietta]	[E.] Harris	1
Goldthwait, Ezekiel *and* [Porter, Stephen & Nath'l.]	Danvers, Mass.	M. Cutler [& J. Dodge]	4 [1]
Goodale, Nathan	Brookfield, Mass.	Foster [R. Putnam & Co.]	2
Goodman, Noah [& Asso:]	Hadley, Mass. [N. Hampton]	[Benjⁿ.] Tupper	1
Gramon [Groman], James, *and* [Windsor, Christopher]	Providence	[William] Corlis	1
Graves, Asa, *and* [Spencer, Joseph]	Hatfield [*no address*]	[Benjⁿ.] Tupper	1
Green, Catharine, *and* [Griffin]	Warwick, R. I. [Marietta]	[A.] Crary	1
" Charles	E. Greenwich, R. I. [Marietta]	"	1
" Elihu [Elihue] & Co., *and* [Elihue & Christ^r. Griffin]	Warwick, R. I.	"	1
" Governor [Wm. Govr.]	"	"	1
" Job	"	"	1
" John	New York	[W.] Sargent	1
" Jonathan	E. Greenwich	Crary	1
" Josiah, *and* [Vaughn, Boon]	Providence	[William] Corlis	1 [0]
" William, 2d [Wm. son of Nathl.], *and* [Griffin]	Warwick	[A.] Crary	1
Greenleaf, Abner	Newburyport	Harris	1
Gridley, William	Boston	[W.] Sargent	1 [0]
Griffin, Samuel	Salem	M. Cutler	1 [0]
Griswould [Griswold], Abiel	Windsor, Conn.	Barlow	1
" Sylvenus [Sylvanus]	"	"	1
Gro[s]venor, Nathan	Pomfret, Conn.	[William] Corlis	1
" Thomas	"	[S. H.] Parsons	1
Guthrie, Joseph	Washington, Conn.	Talmage [Benjⁿ. Talmadge]	2
Hales, William	Gloucester, Mass.	M. Cutler	1 [0]
Hall, Elias [& Asso:]	New Braintree	Foster [R. Putnam & Co.]	2

Halsey, Thomas L.	Providence	[William] Corlis	1
Hamilton, Alexander	New York	[W.] Sargent	5
" " *and* [Stevens, Robert]	Newport	[A.] Crary	1
Hammond, Abijah	New York	[W.] Sargent	5
" [Hammon], William	Newport	[A.] Crary	1
Hanshaw [Henshaw], Samuel	Northhampton, Mass.	[Benjⁿ.] Tupper	1
Hardy, Joseph	New York	[W.] Sargent	1
Harmer, Josiah	Ohio [Philada.]	"	2
Harris, Edward	Newburyport [Kentucky]	[E.] Harris	3 [0]
Hartwell, Ephraim	N. Ipswich, N. H.	M. Cutler	2 [0]
Haskell [Haskill], Elnathan	Boston	[W.] Sargent	1
" Jonathan	Rochester, Mass.	"	1
Haskins [Hoskins], William	Boston	[Jno.] May	1
Hazzard [Hazzard], Ebenezer	New York [Philada]	[W.] Sargent	1
Heart [Hart], Jona., *and* [Abigail]	Berlin, Conn.	[S. H.] Parsons	1
Heartshorn [Hartshorn], Thomas	Salem, Mass.	M. Cutler [& J. Dodge]	1
Heath [& Asso:], Peleg	Hartford, Conn.	Barlow	1
Hedges, David	E. [S.] Hampton	Talmage [Benjⁿ. Tallmadge]	5 [1]
Henderson, Hugh	New York	M. Cutler [& J. Dodge]	2 [2]
Herd [Hird], John [L.]	Ipswich, Mass.	" "	3 [0]
Herredon, David	"	" "	1 [0]
Herrick, John	"	" "	1 [0]
Heylegar, Peter	Boxford	[S. H.] Parsons	5
Heywood [Haywood], Benjⁿ.	St. Croix	Clapp [R. Putnam & Co.]	1
Hildreth, Samuel	Worcester, Mass.	M. Cutler [& J. Dodge]	2
Hilligas, Michael [Hillegas, Mich^l.]	Methuen, Mass. [Methuen]	[W.] Sargent	1
Hine, Abel	New York [Philada.]	Talmage [Benjⁿ. Tallmadge]	1
Hinkl[e]y [& Asso:], Eben^r.	New Milford, Conn.	Barlow	1
Hitchburn, Samuel, *and* [Story, Daniel]	Saybrook, Conn.	M. Cutler [& J. Dodge]	1 [0]
Hitchcock, David	Boston	Foster	1
" Enos	Brookfield, Mass.	[William] Corlis	1

Hobson, Humphrey	Rawley, Mass.	M. Cutler	2 [0]
Holden, John	Warwick, R. I.	Crary	1 [0]
Holroyd, William	Providence	[William] Corlis	1
Horton, Amos	Johnson, R. I. [Jonson]	"	1
Hosmer, Timothy	Farmington, Conn.	Barlow	1
How, Aaron	Conway, Mass. [Marietta]	[Benjn.] Tupper	2 [1]
Howland, Thomas	Newport, R. I.	[A.] Crary	1
Hubbard, Elijah	Middleto[w]n, Conn.	[S. H.] Parsons	1 [0]
" John	Moultonborough	M. Cutler	2
" Nehemiah	Middleto[w]n, Conn.	[S. H.] Parsons	1
Hughes, Thomas	Newport, R. I.	[A.] Crary	1
Humphrey, David	Darby, Conn.	[S. H.] Parsons	1
Humphr[e]y, William	Rehoboth	[William] Corlis	1
Hunt, Elijah	North Hampton	[Benjn.] Tupper	1
Hunter, Henry	Newport, R. I.	[A.] Crary	1
Hunting, Benjamin	S. Hampton	Talmage [Benjn. Tallmadge]	5 [1]
Huntington, Andrew, *and* [Jones J. P. his heirs]	Norwich, Conn. [*no address*]	[S. H.] Parsons	1
" Jedediah, *and* [Lathrop, Azariel]	Norwich, Conn.	"	1
Hurd, John	Boston	[H.] Jackson	1
Ingersol, George	"	"	1
[Jackson, H. & Associates	"	"	1]
" Henry		[W.] Sargent	2 [1]
Jeffers, John	Ohio	"	1
Jenks [Jinks], John, *and* [Joseph]	Providence	[William] Corlis	2
Jewett [Juet], Stephen, *and* [Gilman, I. Benj^a].	Rowley, Mass. [Marietta]	M. Cutler [& J. Dodge]	1
Jones, Daniel	Hartford, Conn.	Barlow	1
" Jno. C.	Boston	[H.] Jackson	5
Joslin, Hope	E. Greenwich, R. I.	Crary	1 [0]
Judd, Elizabeth	Farmington, Conn.	Barlow	1
Judson, David	Washington, Conn.	Talmage [Benjn. Tallmadge]	2
Keith, John, 2nd	Thompson, Conn.	E. Cutler	1 [0]

Name	Location	Agent	Shares	
Kendall, Ephraim	Ipswich, Mass.	M. Cutler	1	[0]
King, Zebulon [Zebulon's heirs]	Newport, R. I.	[A.] Crary	1	
Kirby, Ephraim	Litchfield, Conn.	Talmage [Benjⁿ. Tallmadge]	1	[0]
Kittle, John	Danvers, Mass.	M. Cutler	1	
Knight, Isaac	Plainfield, Conn.	Parsons [Ephraim Cutler 1]	1	
Knowles [Knowls], Charles	Boston [New York]	[Eliphalet] Downer	3	[2]
" Charles	" "	[W.] Sargent	2	[1]
Knox, Henry	New York [Boston]	"	1	
Kuhl, Henry	" " [Philad^a]	"	1	[0]
Labateaux, Hannah	" "	Sargent	1	[0]
Laird, Robert	Newburyport, Mass.	Harris	1	
Lamb, John	Norwich, Conn.	Eliphalet Downer	1	[0]
Lamb & Baker	Brookline, Mass. [Brooklyn]	"	1	[0]
Lambert, Thomas	Rowley, Mass.	"	1	
Langdell, John	Beverly, Mass.	M. Cutler	1	[0]
Lappingwell [Liffingwell], Chris^r.	Norwich, Conn.	"	1	[0]
Larebee [Larraby], Timothy and [Jones J. P. his heirs]	Windham, Conn. [no address]	[S. H.] Parsons	2	[1]
Lathrop, Elijiah, Jur., and [Jones J. P. his heirs]	Norwich, Conn. [no address]	"	1	
Lawrance, Elisha	Killingly, Conn.	E. Cutler	1	[0]
" [Lawrence], John	New York	[W.] Sargent	3	
Leach, Joseph	Manchester, Mass.	M. Cutler	1	[0]
Leavens [Levins], John	Thompson, Conn.	E. Cutler	1	[0]
Leavitt, David, Jur. [& Asso:]	Bethlehem	Talmage [Benjⁿ. Tallmadge]	1	
Le Chapedelain [De Chapedelene], Marq., and [Thomas L. Halsey]	St. Breiux [Providence]	[William] Corlis	5	
Ledyard, Isaac	New York	[W.] Sargent	2	
Lee, Archer [Arthur]	New York [Virginia]	"	2	
Lepet [Lippet], Christopher	Cranston, R. I.	[Sproat &] Dexter	1	
Leucas [Lucas], John	Boston	[H.] Jackson	1	
Levens, Joseph	Thompson, Conn.	E[phraim] Cutler	1	

Littlefield, William	Crary	Newport, R. I.	1 [0]
Livingston, Brockholst	[W.] Sargent	New York	5
" Walter	"	"	3
Loomis, Lebeus [Libbeus]	[Sproat &] Dexter	Cumberland, R. I.	2
Lord, Elisha	[S. H.] Parsons	Pomfret, Conn.	1
" William	"	Saybrook, Conn.	1
Loring, Daniel	Clapp [R. Putnam & Co.]	Sudbury, Mass.	1
Low, John	M. Cutler	Coxhall, Mass.	1 [0]
Lucas, John	[Jno.] May	Boston.	1
Lummis [Loomis], Porter	M. Cutler [& J. Dodge]	Ipswich, Mass.	1
Lumus, John	"	"	1
Lunt, Ezra	[E.] Harris	Newburyport, Mass. [Kentucky]	1 [0]
" " [B. Leigh]	"	"	4 [1]
" " [Call]	"	"	1 [1]
" " [Harris]	"	"	1 [1]
Lyon, Humphrey	[S. H.] Parsons	E. Haddam, Conn.	1
" John	Foster [R. Putnam & Co.]	Le[i]cester, Mass.	1
Lyman, Daniel	[A.] Crary	Newport, R. I.	3 [0]
Mackanon, Will	Parsons	Antigua	5
Macomb [McComb], Alex.	[W.] Sargent	New York	1
" " Eliza.	"	"	5
" " William	"	"	1
Macomber [McComber], Ebenezr.	[Sproat &] Dexter	Providence	1
Malbone, John	Crary	Newport	1 [0]
Manchester, Mathw.	[Sproat &] Dexter	Cranston, R. I.	3
Manning, James, and [Holroyd, William]	[William] Corlis	Providence	1
Marble, Joel	Heywood [R. Putnam & Co.]	Worcester, Mass.	1
Marsh, David W.	[William] Corlis	Providence	1
Marshall, Christopr.	[W.] Sargent	Boston	1
Marshal, Wm.	"	"	1
Mathews, Abel [& Asso:]	[Eliphalet] Downer	Bristol, Conn.	1

Name	Location	Associated		
Mathews, John [& Assoc:]	New Braintree	Foster [R. Putnam & Co.]	1	
Mawney, John	Providence	[Sproat &] Dexter	1	
Mawry [Mowrey], Elisha, Jur.	Smithfield, R. I.	"	1	
Maxwell, Hugh	Heath, Mass.	"	1	[0]
May, Fredk. [Frederik]	Boston	Tupper	1	
" Hy. Knox [Henry K.]	"	[Jno.] May	1	
" John, and [Sargent W.]	"	"	1	
" Jno. W. M. [& Marshall, Wm.]	"	[W.] Sargent	1	
" John, Jur.	"	"	1	
" Joseph	"	"	1	
" "	"	[Jno.] May	1	
" Wm. Rufus [Wilm. R.]	"	"	1	
McCurdy, William	Ohio	[W.] Sargent	1	
Meigs, John	Middleto[w]n	[Jno.] May	1	
Mercer [Mercer], John	Ohio	[W.] Sargent	1	
Miles, Joshua	Brookline, Conn. [Brooklyn]	[S. H.] Parsons	2	
Miller, Nathan	Warren, R. I.	[W] Sargent	1	[0]
Morgan, John	Hartford, Conn.	[S. H.] Parsons	1	
Morton, Jacob	New York	Crary	1	[0]
" Perez, and [Tupper, Huldah]	Boston [Marietta]	[S. H.] Parsons	1	
Morris, James	Litchfield, Conn.	Sargent	1	
" Wm. M.	New York	[Benj^a. Tupper]	3	
Moulton, Willm.	Hempsted, N. H.	Talmage [Benjⁿ. Tallmadge]	2	
" Joseph	Newburyport	[W.] Sargent	2	[1]
Mumford, John	Providence	[E.] Harris	1	[0]
Munro[e], James	Providence	[William] Corlis	1	
" Josiah [& H. White]	Amherst, N. N. [Marietta]	[William] Corlis	1	
Murrey [Murray], John	Glocester [Boston]	[E.] Harris	1	
Newton, John, Jur., and [Lord, Abner]	Colchester, Conn.	[W.] Sargent	1	
Nicholson, James	New York	[S. H.] Parsons	5	[3]
Nightingale & Clarke [Clark]	Providence	[W.] Sargent	5	
		[William] Corlis		

74

Nixon, Thomas	Southborough	Heywood [R. Putnam & Co.]	1
Nurse [Nourse], Joseph	New York [Philada.]	[W.] Sargent	1
Nye, Ichabod	Chesterfield [Marietta]	[Benjn.] Tupper	2 [1]
" Joseph	Harwich	[N.] Freeman	4
" "	Sandwich	"	1
Odiorn [Odion], Thomas	Exeter, N. H.	[E.] Harris	1
Odlin [Odlyn], Dudley, *and* [Gilman, Benj. I.]	"	"	1
Oliver, Alexander [& Asso:]	"	"	2 [1]
" Peter	Conway, Mass. [Belprie]	[Benjn.] Tupper	1
" Robert [& Asso:]	Salem, Mass.	M. Cutler [& J. Dodge]	2
Ohney, Christopher	Chester, Mass. [Marietta]	[Benjn.] Tupper	1
" Cogshall	Providence	[William] Corlis	3
" Jeremiah	Cumberland, R. I. [Ohio]	[Sproat &] Dexter	2
Olyphant, Ann[a]	Providence	[William] Corlis	1
" David	Newport	[A] Crary	3 [2]
Orne, Mary	Wenham	Dodge	1 [0]
Parke [Park], Mat[t]hew, *and* [Thorp, E.]	Boston	M. Cutler [& J. Dodge]	1
Parson[s], Wm. W.	Middletown, Conn.	[S. H.] Parsons	1
Parsons, Enoch	"	"	1
" Joshua, *and* [Miller, Edward]	Palmer [Middletown], Mass.	[S. H.] Parsons	1 [0]
" Mehitabel [to Jno. Niewanger]	Middletown, Conn.	"	1
" Nehem.	Gloucester, Mass.	M. Cutler	1 [0]
" Saml. H. [Samuel H. to Wm.]	Middletown, Conn.	[S. H.] Parsons	5
Patterson, James	Bedford	[Jno.] May	2
Pearson [Parsons], Obadiah	Lynn, Mass.	M. Cutler [& J. Dodge]	1
Peck, William	Providence	[Sproat &] Dexter	1
Peirce [Pierce], David	Glo[u]cester, Mass.	M. Cutler [& J. Dodge]	5 [4]
" Jur.	"	"	5
Perkins, Samuel [G.]	Boston	[Jno.] May	1
Perry, Sylvenus	Killingly, Conn.	E. Cutler	1 [0]
Peters, Andrew [& Asso:]	Mendon, Mass.	[Benjn.] Tupper	2

75

Name	Place	Agent		
Pierce, Jona.	Salem	[M. Cutler & J.] Dodge	1	[0]
" William	"	"	3	[2]
Pierpoint, John	New Haven, Conn.	[S. H.] Parsons	1	
[Pierson, David	South Hampton	Benj. Tallmadge	1]	
Pitman, Sa[u]nders	Providence	[William] Corlis	1	
Phillips, Peter	N. Kingston [No. Kingston]	Corry [Crary]	5	[1]
Platt, Jeremiah	New Haven	[S. H.] Parsons	5	
" Richard	New York	Sargent	5	[0]
Pom[e]roy, Asahel	North Hampton	[Benjⁿ.] Tupper	1	
Porter, Ebenezer, Jur.	Ipswich, Mass.	M. Cutler	1	[0]
[Post, James	So. Hampton	[Benjⁿ.] Tallmadge	1]	
Potter, William	Ipswich, Mass.	M. Cutler	1	[0]
Power, Nicholas	Providence	[William] Corlis	1	
Pratt, Humphrey	Saybrook, Conn.	[S. H.] Parsons	1	
" John	Ohio [Middletown]	[W.] Sargent	2	
Prentice, Jonas	New Haven, Conn. [New York]	[S. H.] Parsons	1	
Putnam, Allen, *and* [Amos Porter]	Danverse, Mass.	M. Cutler [& J.] Dodge	1	[0]
" Edwin	Rutland, Mass. [Marietta]	Foster [R. Putnam & Co.]	1	
" Hara	Middletown, Mass. [Marietta]	Heywood [R. Putnam & Co.]	1	
" Israel, Jur. [Israel]	Brookline, Conn. [Pomfret]	[S. H.] Parsons	4	
" Jethro	Denverse, Mass.	M. Cutler	1	[0]
" Rufus	Rutland, Mass. [Marietta]	[H.] Jackson	2	
" Wm. R.	"	[W.] Sargent	1	
Quegly [Quigly], John [& Asso:]	"	[Benjⁿ.] Tupper	1	
Read [Reed], John, *and* [Miles, John]	Chester	Foster [R. Putnam & Co.]	1	
Redwood, Abraham [Aba. 3d], *and* [Champlin, Christopher]	Rutland	[Benjⁿ.] Tupper	1	
Revera, Jacob R., *and* [Abraham R.]	Newport	Heywood [R. Putnam & Co.]	1	
"	"	[A.] Crary	1	[0]
Reynald, Joseph	E. Greenwich	"	1	[0]

Rice, Henry	Warwick, R. I.	[A.] Crary	1
" Oliver	Sudbury	Heywood [R. Putnam & Co.]	2
" Thomas	Warwick, R. I.	[A.] Crary	1
" William	Sudbury, Mass.	Clapp [R. Putnam & Co.]	1
Richmond, Adam, *and* [Revere,] Abrahm. R.	W. Greenwich, R. I.	[A.] Crary	1
Riddle [Riedls], Henry	Sutton, Mass.	Clapp [R. Putnam & Co.]	2
Rhodes, William	Boston	[Eliphalet] Downer	1
Robards, B. Richard	South Carolina	Sargent	2 [0]
Roger[s], Platt	New York [Fishkill]	[W.] Sargent	1
Rose, John	Pennsylvania	"	1
Ruggles, Nathl.	Roxbury	[Eliphalet] Downer	1
Rumril [Rumrell], Thos.	Newport	[A.] [Crary]	1
Russell, Jona. [Russel], Jonathan	Thompson, Conn.	E[phraim] Cutler	1
" Jos. & Wm.	Providence	[William] Corlis	2
" [Russel], Thomas	Boston	[Jno.] May	5
Sabin, Thomas	Providence	[William] Corlis	1
Sacket, Ananias R.	New York [Fishkill]	[W.] Sargent	1 [0]
Safford, John	Ipswich, Mass.	M. Cutler [& J. Dodge]	1
" Samuel	"	"	2
Sargent, Winthrop	Boston	" [& J. Dodge]	1
" Winthrop *and* [May, John]	Gloucester	Heywood [R. Putnam & Co.]	2 [0]
Savage, Abijah	Boston [N. W. Terr.]	[Jno.] May	1
Sawyer, Nathl.	Boston	[S. H.] Parsons	1
Sayles, David	Middletown	M. Cutler	1 [0]
Scott, Jno. M.	Ipswich, Mass.	[Sproat &] Dexter	1
Scranton, Abrm.	Smithfield, R. I.	[W.] Sargent	1
Scuyler, Derrick [Schuyler, Derick]	Ohio	[S. H.] Parsons	1
Sears, Elisa [Sarah]	Durham	[W.] Sargent	1
Seward, Thomas, *and* [Dyer, John]	Ohio	"	1
	New York	"	2
	Boston		

77

Name	Place	Agent	Count
Shaw, Peter	Beverly, Mass.	M. Cutler [& J. Dodge]	1
Sheffield, Hanah [Hannah]	E. Greenwich [Marietta]	[A.] Crary	1
Shep[p]ard, Enoch	Ohio	[Benj[n].] Tupper	1 [0]
Siexas, Moses	Newport	Crary	1
Sill, David F.	Lyme, Conn.	[S. H.] Parsons	1 [0]
Sizar, William	Chester, Mass.	Tupper	1
Skinner, Timothy	Litchfield	Tallmage [Benj[n]. Tallmadge]	1
Slocum, Benja.	Newport	[A.] Crary	1
" John	"	Crary	1 [0]
Smart, Thomas	Providence	[Sproat &] Dexter	1
Smith, Calvin [& Asso:]	Mendon, Mass.	[Benj[n].] Tupper	1
" Henry	Providence	[William] Corlis	1
" James	Bedford, N. H. [Marietta]	[Jno.] May	1
" Melancton	New York	[W.] Sargent	1
" Paskell [Paschal] N.	"	"	5
" Reuben	Litchfield	Talmage [Benj[n]. Tallmadge]	1
" Stephen	Bristol, R. I.	[William] Corlis	2
Southmaid [Southmayd], Saml.	Watertown, Conn.	Talmage [Benj[n]. Tallmadge]	1
Spauldin, Obad[h].	Killingly, Conn.	E. Cutler	1 [0]
Spraigue [Sprague], John	Dedham	Heywood [R. Putnam & Co.]	2
" John			1
Sproat, Earl	Middleborough, Mass. [Marietta]	[Jno.] May	1
" Ebenezer	Providence [Marietta]	[Sproat &] Dexter	3 [2]
" [Drawn by Coit, Jos., E. Cutler's Agency]	"	"	[1]
Spurr, John			
Stacy, William	New Salem, Mass. [Marietta]	[William] Corlis	1
Stanly, Thos. [& Asso:]	Berlin, Conn. [Marietta]	[Benj[n].] Tupper	4
Stanton, John	Boston	Berlow	1
"	Worcester	Clapp [R. Putnam & Co.]	1
Starr, George	Middletown, Conn.	[S. H.] Parsons	1

78

Name	Location	Agent	Qty
Starr, Josiah	New Milford, Conn.	Talmage [Benjⁿ. Tallmadge]	1
St. Clair, Arthur	Pennsylvania [Ohio]	[W.] Sargent	1
Stephens [Stevens], George	Beverly, Mass.	M. Cutler [& J. Dodge]	1
" Joseph, Jur. [Joseph]	Andover	Clapp [R. Putnam & Co.]	1
" Robt.	Newport	[A.] Crary	1
Sterry, Cyprian	Providence	[William] Corlis	2
Stewart, Archibold [Archibald]	"	"	2
Stillwell [Stilwell], Elias	New Haven	[S. H.] Parsons	1
Stone, Benjamin [& Asso:]	Shrewsbury	Heywood [R. Putnam & Co.]	2
" Jona.	Brookfield [Belprie]	Foster [R. Putnam & Co.]	1 [0]
Storey, Isaac	Marblehead	M. Cutler	1 [0]
" John	Ipswich, Mass.	"	1
" [Story], William, *and* [Daniel]	" [Marietta]	" [& J. Dodge]	2
Story, Daniel	Worcester, Mass. [Marietta]	Heywood [R. Putnam & Co.]	1
Stratten [Stratton], John	Brookline, Mass. [Brooklyn]	[Eliphalet] Downer	1
Strong, Caleb	N. Hampton	Foster [R. Putnam & Co.]	1
" David	Ohio	[W.] Sargent	1
Sturges, Russell [Russel]	Boston	[Jno.] May	1
Sumner [Summer], Job	Georgia	[H.] Jackson	1
Swacy [Swasey], Jos. Jur.	Newburyport	[E.] Harris	1
Swan, Caleb	New York	[W.] Sargent	1
Swart, Evart [Evert] W.	"	[W.] Sargent	1
Swasey, Stephen	Newburyport	[E.] Harris	1
Swift, Heman [pr T. & Co.]	Cornwell [Litchfield], Conn.	Talmage [Benjⁿ. Tallmadge]	2 [1]
" *and* [Nye, Ebenr.]	"	"	[1]
Talcot [Talcot], Gad	Hebron	[S. H.] Parsons	1
[Tallmadge, F. Augustus]	Litchfield	[Benjⁿ.] Tallmadge	1]
Talmage [Tallmadge], Benja.	"	Talmage [Benjⁿ. Tallmadge]	5
" Henry F.	"	"	1
" John [for B. T. & Co.]	Warren [Litchfield]	"	1
" Mary	Litchfield	"	4 [0]

Talmage [Tallmadge], Wm. S.	Litchfield	[Benjⁿ.] Tallmadge	1
Taylor, Nathanl.	New Millford	"	1
Tenney [Tenny], Samuel	Exeter, N. H.	[E.] Harris	1
Tew, William	Newport	[A.] Crary	1
Thayer, Simeon	Providence	[William] Corlis	1
Thomas, Isaih [Pike, Nichs. Assignee]	Worcester, Mass.	Clapp [R. Putnam & Co.]	1
" Joseph	Plymouth, Mass.	[N.] Freeman	1
Thorndike [Thornduke], Israel	Beverly, Mass.	M. Cutler [& J. Dodge]	2 [0]
Thorndike & Larkin	"	"	1
Thurber [Thurbur], Edward, Jur.	Providence	[Sproat &] Dexter	1
" Samuel, Jr.	"	[Sproat &] Dexter	1
Tibbets [Tibbits], Waterman	Warwick, R. I.	[A.] Crary	1
Ticknor, Elisha	Boston	[Jno.] May	1
Til[l]inghast, Daniel	Providence	[Sproat &] Dexter	3
" Nichs. P.	Newport	[A.] Crary	2
" Pardon	Exeter	"	1
Topham, John	W. Greenwich	"	1
Torrey [Terry], Nathan [Nathaniel]	Newport	Barlow	1
" [Torry], William	Infield [Suffield], Conn.	[H.] Jackson	1
Tracey [Tracy], Uriah	Pembrook [Pembroke]	Tallmage [Benjⁿ. Tallmadge]	1
Treadwell, John	Litchfield	M. Cutler [& J. Dodge]	2
Troop, Benjamin	Salem, Mass.	[S. H.] Parsons	1
True, Jabez [Doct^r]	Hamstead, N. H. [Marietta]	[E.] Harris	2 [1]
Trumball, Jona.	Lebanon. Conn.	[S. H.] Parsons	2
Tupper, Anselm	Chesterfield [Marietta]	[Benjⁿ.] Tupper	1
" Benjamin	" Marietta	"	4 [2]
" " heirs	" "	"	1
" " Jur.	" "	"	1
" Edward W.	" "	"	1
Turner, Peter	E. Greenwich	[A.] Crary	3

Name	Location	Reference	Count
Tyler, Danl. Jun.			1
" Dean			1 [0]
Underwood, Robt.	Brookline, Conn. [Brooklyn]	[S. H.] Parsons	2 [0]
Vernon, Samuel	Haverhill, Mass.	M. Cutler	1 [0]
" William	New York [Philadela]	[W.] Sargent	2 [0]
Vernum, J. M.	Newport	Crary	3 [0]
" [Varnum], J[ames] M. for Saml. Fowler	"	[A.] Crary	1
	"	Crary	
	"	[A.] Crary	
Wadsworth, Benja.	Danvas [Danvers]	M. Cutler [& J. Dodge]	3
" Elijah	Litchfield	Talmadge [Benjn. Tallmadge]	3
Wainwood, Godfrey	Newport	Crary	1 [0]
Waldo, John	Boston	[Eliphalet] Downer	1
Wald[r]on, John	Bristol, R. I.	[William] Corlis	1
Wales, Ebenezer	Dorchester	[Jno.] May	1
Walker, John	Rehoboth	[William] Corlis	1
" Joseph	Stratford, Conn.	[S. H.] Parsons	1
" Robt.	"	"	1
Walkutt [Walcut], Thomas	Boston	[W.] Sargent	1
Ward, Samuel	Warwick, R. I.	Crary	2 [0]
Wardwell, Saml. [To G. Green]	Bristol, R. I.	[William] Corlis	1
Warner, Jona.	Hardwich	Foster	1 [0]
Waters, Nathl.	Ward, Mass.	Clap	1 [0]
Waterhous [Watrous], Daniel	Colchester	[S. H.] Parsons	1
Waterman, Nathaniel [Nathan]	Providence	[William] Corlis	1
Waterous [Watrous], Jno. R.	Gloucester, Mass. [Colchester]	[S. H.] Parsons	1
Watson, John	E. Win[d]sor	Barlow	2
Webb, Samuel B.	New York	Sargent	1 [0]
Wells, James	Hartford	Barlow	1 [0]
" Thomas, 2d.	Hopkinton	Crary	1 [0]
Wetzell [Wotzell], Mat[t]hew	New York	[W.] Sargent	1
Wheaton, Nathl.	Providence	[William] Corlis	1

Name	Place	Agent		
Wheaton, William	Providence	[Sproat &] Dexter	1	
Whipple, Abram	Cranston [Marietta]	"	2	[0]
" Jesse	Killingly, Conn. [Thompson]	E[phraim] Cutler	1	
" John	Ipswich, Mass.	M. Cutler	1	[0]
" Saml.	"	"	1	[0]
White, Haffield	Danvas, Mass. [Marietta]	" " [& J. Dodge]	2	
Whiteridge, Josiah	Danvers	" " "	1	[0]
" Richd.	Danvas	" " "	1	[0]
Whiting, Zenus	Beverly, Mass.	" " "	1	[0]
Whit[e]man, Eliza. [Elizabeth]	Newport	[A.] Crary	1	
" [Whitmore, Nath.]	Newburyport	E. Harris	1]	
Whitmash, Micah	E. Greenwich	Crary	1	[0]
Whitmore, Amos	Newbury	[E.] Harris	1	
" Ebenr.	Newburyport	Harris	1	[0]
" Nathl.	"	[E.] Harris	1	
Whitney, Elisha	Roxbury	[Elaphalet] Downer	2	
" " and [Burley], William	Ipswich	M. Cutler [& J. Dodge]	1	
Whitridge, Wm.	Danvas	M. Cutler	1	[0]
[Wickham,] Thomas	E. Hampton	[Benjn.] Tallmadge	1]	
Wichham, Wm.	New York	[W.] Sargent	1	
Wilkinson, Joseph	Smithfield, R. I.	[Sproat &] Dexter	1	
Willard, Joseph [Joseph Peat]	Cambridge	M. Cutler [& J. Dodge]	1	
Williams, Abram	Sandwich	[N.] Freeman	1	
" Jeremiah	Boston	[W.] Sargent	1	
" Jona.	"	M. Cutler [& J. Dodge]	2	
" Joseph	Springfield	[W.] Sargent	2	
" Nathan	Tolland, Conn.	Parsons [Barlow]	1	
" Robt. Jur.	Boston	M. Cutler [& J. Dodge]	2	
Willis, John P.	"	[Jno.] May	1	[0]
" [Wyllys], Saml.	Hartford	Barlow	1	

Wilson, George [& heirs]	Killingly, Conn.	E[phraim] Cutler	1
Windsor, Joseph	Glocester, R. I.	[William] Corlis	1
Wisenfelts [Wyzenfitz], Frederick, *and* [Charra, James]	New York	[W.] Sargent	1
Woodbury, Jno.	Salem	M. Cutler	1 [0]
Wyatt [Wyat], Lamuel	Rehoboth, Mass.	[William] Corlis	1
Wyman, Abel	Woburn, Mass.	M. Cutler	1 [0]
Z[e]iglar, David	Ohio	[W.] Sargent	2

ORIGINAL PROPRIETORS OF GALLIOPOLIS, OHIO

Following is a copy of a document accompanying the returns of a survey and partition of lands in Ohio found in the General Land Office, Drafting Division, Washington, D. C., while this writing was in preparation. The document is a ms. letter folded and stitched in a leather book of field notes bearing this inscription stamped on the cover:

> A Survey of the Tract of Land
> Granted by Act of Congress
> to the French Inhabitants
> at Gallipolis.
> List of Actual Settlers &c.
> Rufus Putnam's Letter, dated
> 12th May 1796.[99]

Superscription on the letter: Oliver Wolcott, Esquire, Secretary of the Treasury of the United States.

Sir   MARIETTA May 12th 1796

By the papers herewith enclosed you will perceive that the Lands proposed by the Act of Congress of the Third of March 1795 to be granted to the French inhabitants of Gallioppolis, are surveyed and assigned to the several persons entitled thereto (as I trust) agreeably to the intention of the afore-mentioned act, and your instructions of the Twenty-ninth of September 1795.

Mr Martin[100] arrived at Galliopolis the Second of November and within a few days after commenced his survey; which which he completed as soon as could be expected, but from an ill state of health, as he informs me, he was not able to make the returns before the 25th ult. On reciveing them I proceeded to Galliopolis, as soon as I could with convenience, and the several lots were assigned to individuals on the Third instant in maner certified in the list of Drafts, and I beleave the whole business has been conducted to the satisfaction of all concerned.

Mr Martin states the distence run in executing this survey to be 125 miles 72 chains & 98 links, and the time necesarily employed in making duplicate plans & certificates 34 days. My agreement with Mr Martin was to execute the survey at "the rate of three Dollars permile for every mile actually run including the pay of assistents and all expense of the survey And for the makeing Duplicate Plans with Certificate of the Courses Distances and boundaries; two dollars per day for the necessary time. I have furnished Mr Martin with a certificate of the compensation contracted for, also that he has executed the surveys agreeably to the Act of Congress and returned Duplicate Plans Certificates &c., to me: but have referred him to the Treasury Department for auditing his accounts which I presume was your expectation

> I am with great respect & esteam
> Sir Your obedient servant
> RUFUS PUTNAM

OLIVER WOLCOTT, Esqr

---

[99] Cf. Land Laws of the U. S., p. 223.
[100] Capt. Absalom Martin, Surveyor, who represented New Jersey in the original survey of the Seven Ranges of Townships, 1785-88.

A List of the French inhabitants and Actual Settlers of the Town of Gallipolis; being males above eighteen years of age or widows, who were, in pursuance of instructions from Oliver Wolcott Esqr, Secretary of the Treasury of the United States, to Rufus Putnam: by him assertained to be within the said Town of Gallipolis on the First day of November 1795 agreeably to the second section of an Act of Congress passed the Third Day of March 1795, entitled: An Act to Authorize a Grant of Lands to the French inhabitants of Gallipolis, and for other purposes therein mentioned, Together with the number of the Lot assigned (by lot) to each settler prefixed to his or her name, in a Tract of Twenty Thousand acres of Land being part of Twenty-four Thousand acres surveyed agreeably to the Third Section of said Act and is subdivided into Lots, &c agreeably to the Fourth Section of the same Act.

Lot No.	Names Drawn against	Lot No.	Names drawn against
1	Matthew Berthelot Senr[101]	35	John Francis Gobeau
2	Nicholas Thevenin	36	John Julius Lemoyne
3	John Baudot	37	Peter Duteil
4	Peter Matthew Chandivert	38	Lewis Joiteau
5	Francis Valodin	39	Agustus Chereau
6	William Duduit	40	Peter John Desnoyers
7	Nicholas Hurteaux	41	Marin Dupert
8	Peter Lewis Leclerc J^r	42	Agustin Leclercq Senr
9	Peter Marret Senr	43	Nicholas Lambert
10	Michael Mazure	44	John Brouin
11	Lewis Ambrose Lacour	45	Agustin Leclercq J^r
12	Lewis Berthe	46	Anthony Philipeau
13	John Baptist Ginat	47	Anthony Henry Mingun
14	Lewis Anthony Francis Cei.	48	Lewis Peter Leclere Senr
15	Andrew Lecrouix	49	Mary Magdalen Brunier, widow
16	John Baptist Berthond	50	Remy Thierry Quiffe
17	Francis Davous	51	Peter Magnier
18	Anthoney Bartholomew Due	52	Matthew Ibert
19	Philip Agustus Pithoud	53	J^{no} Baptist Nicholas Tillaye
20	Stephen Bastide	54	Anthony Claudius Vincent
21	John Parmantier	55	John Gilbert Petit
22	Martinus Vandenbernden	56	Lewis Augustin Lemoyne
23	Nicholas Prioux	57	Basil Joseph Marret
24	Francis Alexander Larquilhon	58	Joseph Michau
25	Nicholas Questel	59	Joseph Dazet
26	Christopher Etienne	60	Michael Craufaz
27	Francis Duverger	61	Francis D'hébècourt
28	Claudius Chartier Duflique	62	John Francis Perrey
29	Nicholas Petit	63	Claudius Romaine Menager
30	John Baptist Letailleur	64	Peter Richon
31	Claudius Berthelot	65	Peter Matry
32	Francis Charles Duteil	66	Peter Serre
33	John Peter Romain Bureau	67	Francis Marion
34	James Francis Laurent	68	Peter Marret, J^r

[101] The numbered lots are shown on the map accompanying the document.

Lot No.	Names drawn against	Lot No.	Names drawn against
69	Francis Winar Joseph Devacht	81	Joachin Pignolet
70	Nicholas Charles Visinier	82	Anthony Vibert
71	Agustus Waldemard Mentelle	83	John Lewis Violet
72	Stephen Chandivert	84	Peter Laffillard
73	Peter Robert Maquet	85	Peter Chabot
74	Stephen Willermi	86	Peter Thomas Thomas
75	John Baptist Ferard	87	Michael Chanterel
76	Francis Alexander Dubois	88	Francis Carteron
77	John Lewis Maldan	89	Claudius Cadot
78	Francis Mennessiers	90	Lewis Victor Vonschriltz
79	Peter Serrot	91	Peter Francis Agustin Leclercq
80	Anthony Francis Saugrain	92	Peter Ferard

I hereby certify that the foregoing numbers of Lots were severally drawn against the Names before which they respectively stand; at Galliopolis on the Third Day of May 1796, by a committee of the inhabitants acting under my imediate superintendence, and that I have inscribed each proprietors Name on his Lot Drawn as aforesaid in two Plats of the survey made by Absalom Martin.   RUFUS PUTNAM.

In another book marked "A." is a plat of the subdivision with each lot bearing the proprietor's name, and inscribed:

A Map of the Tract of Land granted by the Honble the Congress of the United States to the French Inhabitants of Galliopolis, divided agreeably to the Act and according to the Instructions from General Rufus Putnam into.

      1 Tract of   4,000 Mr Gervais[102]
      92 lots of 217 $\frac{89}{100}$ Acres 20,000

Surveyed by
 Absalom Martin   Acres 24,000
April 9 1796.

By an act of Congress passed June 25, 1798 (Land Laws of U. S., 1810, p. 225), Stephen Monot, Lewis Anthony Carpentier, Lewis Vimont, Francis Valton, Lewis Philip A. Fichow, Anthony Maquet, Margaret G. C. Champaigne wife of Peter A. Laforge, and Maria I. Dalliez wife of Peter Luc, inhabitants of Galliopolis, who were prevented from obtaining their proportion of the land granted by the act of March 3, 1795, received each an eighth equal part of a tract of 2200 acres on the Ohio River "beginning at the lower corner" of the Galliopolis tract.

[102] John Gabriel Gervais.

www.ingramcontent.com/pod-product-compliance
Lightning Source LLC
Chambersburg PA
CBHW030558080526
44585CB00012B/418